NUMEROLOGY AWAKENING:

Decode Your Destiny and Master Your Life through Tarot, Astrology and Numerology to Discover Who You Are and Predict Your Future through the Magic of Numbers

By
Michelle Northrup

© Copyright 2019 by Michelle Northrup - All rights reserved.

This book is provided with the sole purpose of providing relevant information on a specific topic for which every reasonable effort has been made to ensure that it is both accurate and reasonable. Nevertheless, by purchasing this book you consent to the fact that the author, as well as the publisher, are in no way experts on the topics contained herein, regardless of any claims as such that may be made within. As such, any suggestions or recommendations that are made within are done so purely for entertainment value. It is recommended that you always consult a professional prior to undertaking any of the advice or techniques discussed within.

This is a legally binding declaration that is considered both valid and fair by both the Committee of Publishers Association and the American Bar Association and should be considered as legally binding within the United States.

The reproduction, transmission, and duplication of any of the content found herein, including any specific or extended information will be done as an illegal act regardless of the end form the information ultimately takes. This includes copied versions of the work both physical, digital and audio unless express consent of the Publisher is provided beforehand. Any additional rights reserved.

Furthermore, the information that can be found within the pages described forthwith shall be considered both accurate and truthful when it comes to freely available information and general consent. As such, any use, correct or incorrect, of the provided information will render the Publisher free of responsibility as to the actions taken outside of their direct purview. Regardless, there are zero scenarios where the original author or the Publisher can be deemed liable in any fashion for any damages or hardships that may result from any of the information discussed within.

Finally, any of the content found within is ultimately intended for entertainment purposes and should be thought of and acted on as such. Due to its inherently ephemeral nature nothing discussed within should be taken as an assurance of quality, even when the words and deeds described herein indicated otherwise. Trademarks and copyrights mentioned within are done for informational purposes in line with fair use and should not be seen as an endorsement from the copyright or trademark holder.

TABLE OF CONTENTS

Introduction 1

Chapter 1 *Numerology* 4

Chapter 2 *Your Personal Numbers* 11

Chapter 3 *Success Numbers And Practice* 30

Chapter 4 *Astrology* 39

Chapter 5 *The Zodiac* 61

Chapter 6 *Your Astrology* 69

Chapter 7 *Tarot* 78

Chapter 8 *Forecasting* 88

Chapter 9 *Numerology, Astrology and Tarot: The Connection* 93

Conclusion 96

Description 97

INTRODUCTION

Congratulations on purchasing *Numerology Awakening* and thank you for doing so.

The following chapters will discuss numerology and how numbers affect our daily lives regardless of whether or not we acknowledge them. It's no secret that numbers play an important role in our current society and the history of civilization. These symbols are not only used to count and measure the world around us but also are representative of deeper meanings.

In our current society, we value only the tangible. Materialism and scientific explanation rule our perspective on the nature of reality, leaving much speculation to more subtle energies and spiritual qualities of the world. Not everything can be proven in a laboratory, but this doesn't mean that these things aren't real. Many people take the simpler route of accepting that nothing exists past what you can see and touch, but just as many feel that there is much more to our existence than what science can manage in a lab. If you're reading this, or even a bit curious on the subjects at hand, then you are more than likely one of the latter.

Numbers may be taken for granted as simple ways to organize and interpret the tangible world, but what about the intangible? Many cultures from all around the world use numbers as ways to learn about the unknown, to examine patterns in nature and the human mind. You may be able to count higher and higher for an infinite amount of time, but to many ancient societies, these huge numbers are no more complex than single digits. The numbers 1 – 9 are seen as the only true numbers and all other numbers are simply repetitions on these single digits. This book aims to examine these patterns and teach the reader how to use these patterns to their advantage.

Numbers are powerful. They are used in every aspect of life; all jobs and recreational activities require numbers to be used. All inventions and technologies would not be possible without mathematics and other use of these symbols. We see unlucky numbers in some cultures; we see certain dates and other powerful meanings being assigned to numbers. This is number's influence on the tangible world, but what about the deeper lesser-known aspects of the numbers themselves? Are humans giving the numbers their power through cultural progress and attention? Or do these numbers have a will of their own?

Each number has a personality, a certain set of behaviors that influence the entire natural world. The more subtle nature of numbers is rarely studied in contemporary sciences, left to be ridiculed as superstition from old cultures that simply didn't have the advanced technology to know otherwise. With even a little practice of numerology, an observant mind can see that there is more going on with these powerful symbols and ideas. With these practices, we can find the synchronicities and relationships of seemingly unrelated events. This helps us better understand our world and not blame ourselves or others for strange events but gives us another outlet beyond science that natural forces work within. This knowledge is invaluable. Not only does this open doors to more emotional balance but also offers a greater awareness of what's going on around us.

Here in this book, we aim to open the door for beginners to use numerology to better their lives and understand more deeply the nature of reality. We will be able to define our perspective on our own terms and find the subtle energies around us using numerology. But numerology is an incomplete practice. To fully put these practices into play we need other esoteric studies as well.

Astrology and tarot have numerology inherently built into their systems. While these two practices are growing more and more popular each year, they bring numerology with them to fill in gaps that need numbers to be described. These systems acknowledge the divine relationship between numbers and humans. These arts have been used for centuries for divination and communion with the mystical and unknown, and today in the 21st century see a growing popularity, even in a science-based world. While you can take a lot of knowledge from the numbers themselves, adding astrological and tarot systems for forecasting future events make for a trifecta of powerful divination.

With this book, you hold a powerful key to unlocking your potential to take control of your destiny. You can better prepare yourself for important events that otherwise may have been unexpected. You can see into your own behavior and habits, gaining insight into your own personal growth. You can even find ways to answer tough questions and navigate the rough paths that life tends to challenge us with. These are just a few examples of the immense potential that numerology, astrology and tarot can offer.

So these practices have been abandoned by the majority of the western world, but here we aim to change this. You now begin your new journey to transform your perspective, to empower yourself and to balance your life with numerology. Be respectful and humble as you approach these practices; they are ancient and very transformative. And always keep in mind that this is your path, listen to your heart and do what feels right to you when using these arts to your advantage.

There are plenty of books on this subject on the market, thanks again for choosing this one! Every effort was made to ensure it is full of as much useful information as possible. Please enjoy!

CHAPTER 1
Numerology

Numerology has been used for centuries as a means to access the divine through the use of numbers. Seeing natural patterns in numbers and recognizing their influence is a big part of this practice. As you begin this journey be aware of the patterns around you in everyday life. It is one thing to use numbers as a means of measuring or counting, but to see their presence in all aspects of life takes a heightened awareness and great observation skills.

What is Numerology?

Numerology techniques can be used for a multitude of various reasons. Some use the patterns in numbers to make decisions about investments and to draw scientific influences from the numbers. Some may use the patterns to analyze the economy and its ups and downs over a long period of time. For our intents and purposes in this book, we use the traditional definition of numerology as it was used by mystics and students long ago, as a way to build relationships with numbers as a means to connect with the divine. This belief adheres to the idea that there is an inherent mystical relationship between numbers and certain events that take place around the world as well as in our personal lives. These studies also believe that there is a mystical numerical value to many things including; words, names, thoughts, planets and individuals themselves.

Within these esoteric beliefs, it is thought that there are only nine numbers. 1,2,3,4,5,6,7,8, and 9 are thought to be the only actual numbers that exist, while any number 10 and above is simply the base nine numbers repeating themselves. This is seen by the simple act of taking the number 10, adding its digits together (1+0=1) and having a sum of 1. If you were to continue, you would see that each subsequent number adds up to the pattern of 1, 2,3,4,5,6,7,8 and 9.

Example: Eleven; 1+1=2, Twelve; 1+2=3, Thirteen; 1+3=4

This pattern carries on infinitely. And this technique is the very basic principle of numerology; adding digits together to receive a single digit value. While numbers with more than one digit do have their complex personalities on their own, by reducing the value down to one digit, we can see its most basic aspects. You can essentially take any number and reduce them to a single digit using this technique and have meaningful insight into what that number may mean to you or the greater world.

This brings up the question of zero as well. In many numerological systems, zero is not considered a number. It is thought of as infinite, rather than having a value. Zero has no beginning or end; it is empty. While zero is still used to symbolize value, it needs another number before it to have any value at all. This is why zero is left out of the base numbers, and of course, when reducing numbers to single digits zero is zero.

The actual use of the word numerology is fairly new. Dating back to as early as 1907 in the English language, numerology was popular during the Victorian era in the western world, but we see with is expansive history that numerology has been practiced for centuries, potentially even before the use of writing. With more recent surges in popularity, numerology has a history and contemporary power that is validated more so each day with its successful use.

This study of numbers reveals to us the habits and tendencies of our personality. We can also apply this to other's personalities. The numbers reflect a certain pattern that we seem to naturally adhere to. It is thought that the vibrations of certain sounds have a numerical value, and since life is a series of vibrations every event potentially can be attributed to a number. As far as your personal numerology these numbers will reveal an exceptional amount of detail about your purpose in life, your aspirations, and how you may find your true calling. Numerology can be used to time big events in life, or better prepare for them as well. With all the wonderful uses many feel like it is too good to be true or too complicated. It may seem complex, but most things in life are. Whether you're trying to become an expert in numerology or just want to improve a few aspects of your life, it is good to consider its history and use.

Historical use of numerology

We know that numerology has been practiced for centuries, but we can't quite pinpoint its exact beginnings. Like so many other esoteric and occult practices it is impossible to know its exact origin, but we can analyze our earliest records of numerology. It is to be expected that we find these techniques used in early civilizations. There has been evidence discovered in written records of the use of numerology in Egypt. Even earlier we see that the Chaldean system of Babylon uses numerology. Experts agree that the Chaldean system was greatly influenced by Hebrew numerology. More recent use of numerology has been discovered in China and Japan dating back just a few thousand years.

While these old civilizations were using numerology, it is tough to know how broad the scope of their studies actually was. Modern-day numerology is often attributed to the writings of the popular Greek philosopher Pythagoras. Pythagoras' work with numbers and mathematics have influenced modern day use in an incredible way. His ideas that numbers were an important role in any event or relationship have formed mathematical thought to what it has become today. Pythagoras felt that it was the duty of the mind to contemplate the numerical relationships between all things.

As time went on and the influence of Christianity spread rampantly across the western world, certain practices were condemned, including numerology. Numerology, along with astrology and tarot, were classified as magic and considered to be evil practices. This religious suppression of the magical arts created a huge shift in the use of numerology. Many were forced to work in private or be subject to the influence of numbers without even knowing it. Even though the power of the church did well in eliminating numerology practices, the Bible itself has heavy use of numbers and numerological practices. It is safe to say that the influence of numbers is unavoidable.

We can learn a lot about the popular history of numerology, but we learn even more by analyzing how numerology was used in different cultures. One of the more common practices using numbers to assign a value to certain sounds or letters of the alphabet. This is found in many ancient cultures, notably in Kabbalah and the Hebrew language where the symbol's numerical value is just as important as the sound it makes when spoken. There are many differing opinions about how these different systems are translated into English with their numerical value. Below are some examples of alphabets and their numerological values.

Latin Alphabetic Values

1 – a, j, s   2 – b, k, t   3 – c, l, u

4 – d, m, v   5 – e, n, w   6 – f, o, x

7 – g, p, y   8 – h, q, z   9 – i, r

Indian or Vedic Alphabetic Values

1 – a, I, j, q, y   2 – b, k, r   3 – c, g, l, s

4 – d, m, t   5 – e, h, n, x   6 – u, v, w

7 – o, z   8 – f, p   9 – i, r

Pythagorean Alphabetic Values

1 – a, j, s   2 – b, k, t   3 – c, l, u

4 – d, m, v   5 – e, n, w   6 – f, o, x

7 – g, p, y   8 – h, q, z   9 – i, r, x

These two systems are the most common systems that have been translated into English. Other languages rely heavily on the sounds themselves and are more complex than the English alphabet; this makes it difficult to account for sounds that are found in English but not in other languages and vice versa. Also, the use of numerical values is different in many languages, based more on the sounds and other qualities like whether or not the word is a homophone or has other attributes, like an unlucky history or connotation.

We see other attributions as well besides alphabets. Assigning numbers to the planets and other heavenly bodies is a very popular idea found in many cultures as well. These numerical values are not all identical across the board though. Below are numerical values found in Indian or Vedic numerology, as well as Kabbalah numerology.

The numbers Indian

1 - Sun
2 - Moon
3 - Jupiter
4 - Rahu
5 - Mercury
6 - Venus
7 - Ketu
8 - Saturn
9 – Mars

Kabbala
1. The Sun
2. The Moon (New)
3. Jupiter
4. The Earth or Sun
5. Mercury.
6. Venus
7. The Moon (Full)
8. Saturn

Tree of life

1 - Pluto
2- Uranus
3 - Saturn
4 – Jupiter
5 - Mars
6 - Sun
7- Venus
8 - Mercury
9 – Moon
10 – Earth

So we see here how the numerical value of certain things can be viewed through many lenses. Depending on the context these values can be used successfully. There is no one way to view the numbers; they exist on levels even beyond our perspective as humans in modern times. It is wise to use a numerology system that feels right to you. Pick a system that may be in line with your ancestry or whichever one may be the most attractive to you.

Contemporary use of numerology

Today numerology is used by a wide variety of people in many different forms. We see spiritually minded people as well as the less spiritually inclined building new relationships with numbers and their natural influence. There is a popular uprising of occult practices which has led to numerology's modern acceptance as well. New age groups, occultists, neo-pagans, and even atheists have all found members of their respective perspectives using numerology and astrology to improve their lives and develop a new understanding as to the true nature of reality. Even more traditional religious sects still use ancient numerology practices in their daily lives.

It is also common in our technologically advanced world to really question how numerology may work. While there is very little investment in trying to validate these practices, you will find very few studies to attempt to. The mysterious nature of these esoteric ideas and practices is something that was of no concern to students in ancient times. If the techniques worked then, that was proof enough. When developing a worldview that is trying to fit the validity of numerology into its philosophy be open minded.

Many believe the numbers themselves to have life and power, whether in our world or another. Some feel that the number's power comes from complex patterns that are built into nature and affect us that way. Others still feel there is spiritual intelligence that works through numbers to communicate with us. However, you want to explain your work to keep in mind that no one really knows for sure.

While many people have had fun calculating their personal numerology online, rarely does their practice go beyond this small venture into onto the numerology path. It is fun to memorize your personal numbers, but actually working with them is where the real empowerment comes into play. Not unlike someone stating their astrological sun sign, "Oh I'm a Pisces so ..." many do the same with their personal numerology.

It is recommended that if you are taking a serious approach to empowering yourself through numerology that you refrain from getting caught up in vague understandings and umbrella terms. If you truly wish to gain insight from these practices it is best suggested that you approach them with humility and focus on what actually works for you rather than what's popular in our society. No one system or technique will work for everyone, find your style and niche and use it. With this in mind let's move onto how to calculate your personal numerology.

CHAPTER 2
Your Personal Numbers

Calculating your personal numerology will give you a single digit number that is representative of certain habits and patterns that are inherent in your life. These numbers don't necessarily define who you are, but instead offers insight into your natural numerical makeup. With these numbers, you can study the qualities that the number is attributed to have, following a trail of insight that will not only help you learn about yourself but also help you learn about the subtle nature of numerical energies that are a part of everyday life.

Your personal numerology is closely connected to astrology as we will learn in subsequent chapters, but for now, we will focus on the number's personality itself rather than planetary attributes. As you learn about your personal numbers, you will be intrigued to see how your number relates to other numbers. You will begin to unlock the secrets of each number and soon realize their personalities and natural qualities. Although you will have a more personal relationship with your own numbers, you will soon find out that each number relies on the others to be complete. This symbiosis is another key to the secrets of numbers and their influences on our world and each other.

How to calculate your numerology

Calculating your personal numerology is quite simple. But do not be fooled by the simplicity of nine single-digit numbers, these numbers hold the keys to many secrets that humanity has been seeking for centuries. Although there are many different aspects of your life that a numerical value can be calculated for, we will focus on three main numbers. The Birth path or destiny number, the psychic number, and your name number. These are the three main numbers found in modern numerology that are calculated for individuals.

As mentioned above the calculations of numerology are reduced to a single digit number. For the calculations in this chapter we are focusing on the more traditional systems, we will expand on more modern calculations in later chapters.

It needs to be reiterated that these descriptions below are basic guidelines for each number, how it plays into your personal life will depend on other variables as well. We will explain this with more depth in the following astrology and tarot chapters.

Birth path number

The birth path numbers, also known as destiny numbers, is the number that relates to how others see you. This number is synonymous with the way the world sees you in general. As you progress through life, you may face many challenges, the more successful you are at facing these challenges and learning from them, the more your destiny number becomes apparent and influential.

The birth path number is very important and influential throughout your life, but many numerology systems believe that this number really starts showing its face during midlife, so ages 35 or 40 onward. Some even view midlife crises as their destiny number making itself apparent in various ways.

The birth path number is thought to be the most important overall number in numerology since it plays such an integral role throughout your entire life. Calculating your birth path or destiny number requires all the digits in your entire date of birth to be added together and reduced. This means the day, month and year. For example, if your birthday October 23, 1980, you would add together October's number on the calendar, 10, plus 23 and 1980. It would look like this:

$$1+0+2+3+1+9+8+0=24$$

Add the digits together and you get the number 24. Now add the digits in 24 together.
$$2+4=6$$

In this example, six is our destiny or birth path number. At this point, you would use the chart below to see what qualities six represents and contemplate how six has played a role in your life throughout the years this number is your main number when it comes to not only your adult life but all of your life. You may find that certain days that are 'sixes,' for example, the 6th, 15th or 24th, of any given month may be favorable or important days for you. Analyze your life and see where six has popped up and try to find any patterns that relate to six in your life.

Psychic number

The psychic number is found most commonly in Indian and Vedic systems. This number represents how you see yourself. It's the number that reveals your desires and dreams; it is almost like a mirror for you to look into. This number is thought to be the most powerful during early life before middle age. The psychic number can reveal your natural talents and plays a big role in youthful socializing. This number will be obvious in the way you carry yourself day to day in the first thirty years of your life.

The psychic number is calculated simply by adding the digits of the day you were born together. So if you were born on October 23rd, you would just add the 23 together.

$$2+3=5$$

In this example, the psychic number is five. Here we would then go to the chart below and see what qualities are attributed to the number five. We can see five have played a role in our early lives, looking back at certain ages that are 'fives' such as the year you were 5 years old, or the year you were 14 years old. Days that are 'fives' may be favorable or important as well, so any given day of the month that is the 5th, 14th or 23rd.

Name Number

The name number is the numerical value of your name. While many sources online have different names for this number, often destiny or soul number, we are going to keep it simple with our three main numbers and keep this one labeled as the 'name number.' This number is thought to represent your relationships with other people. Imagine how often you hear your name throughout your life; this vibration of sound most certainly has an effect on you in some subtle way. By assigning a numerical value, we can better understand our name's influence on our lives.

While this number is very important throughout your life, it can be altered throughout your life. Consider people with nicknames or people who have name changes. These people are drastically altering the influence of the numbers in their numerology. So you may have many name numbers throughout your life, it is agreed upon by numerologists that the full name given to you at birth and its numerological value is an important number to always consider throughout your life. Although if your name number isn't a favorable number with your other numerology or it clashes with your personal astrology, then you may consider getting a name changed or assuming a new name that is favorable. We see these name changes in many cultures; some new age teachers take on different names. Some people abandon their given name to detach from religious traditions, and others get married and find a more suitable name to adhere to. If you are changing your name calculate your name number to make sure you are giving yourself a more favorable name.

Calculating your name number will require a system of the alphabet to numerical value translation. You can find many calculators online to do this. For our purposes here we will use the Latin alphabetic values:

$$1 - a, j, s \qquad 2 - b, k, t \qquad 3 - c, l, u$$

$$4 - d, m, v \qquad 5 - e, n, w \qquad 6 - f, o, x$$

$$7 - g, p, y \qquad 8 - h, q, z \qquad 9 - i, r$$

Take the letters of your name. In this example, we will use Christopher.

C=3, H=8, R=9, I=9, S=1, T=2, O=6, P=7, H=8, E=5, R=9

$$3+8+9+9+1+2+6+7+8+5+9=67$$
$$6+7=13$$

$$1+3=4$$

In this example, the name Christopher reduces to a numerical value of four. Here we would go to the number charts below and find four to see what attributes four represents in the sphere of numerology. This would be similar to saying that as often as the name Christopher is used the influence of four is just as common. Each time this name is heard or written, then you have 'four' influence.

When calculating these important numbers be aware of how often you see certain numbers. If you have an abundance of 'fours', then you may have unbalanced numerology leaning toward the personality of four. It is thought that whenever two numbers are added together to make nine that they are complementary to each other. So to compliment four, you would want more 'five' influence since 4+5=9. So, respectively these pairs of numbers are opposites; 1 and 8, 2 and 7, 3 and 6, 4 and 5. The number nine does not have an opposite and is considered quite different in attitude compared to the other numbers. See the number 9 section for more information on this.

Also accompanying each number is their ruling planet, color and day. These specific things are favorable for that certain number. So if you have a heavy '1' influence, you may balance out and manage its influence through work with its respective planet, the sun, or by planning certain events on Sundays. Wearing the color of a certain number will bring more of its influence into your personal sphere. Be thoughtful when approaching these workings, if you have too much of one number, then wearing or working with its opposite will help balance out the energy. Use the planets, colors and days to familiarize yourself with all nine numbers.

The Numbers

So we have seen that calculating our numerology is relatively simple. Now we need to familiarize ourselves with the numbers and their respective personalities. Keep in mind that no particular number is good or bad; there is a balance to every number. How it relates to you and interacts with other numbers creates adverse or favorable situations. Below will be a list of the numbers and how they fit into the calculations of the birth path, psychic and name numbers. The attribute below is predominantly using tradition numerological systems.

1 – ONE

Planet: Sun – Color: Yellow Golden White – Day: Sunday

The number one overall is an energetic and confident one. Leadership roles are important as well as creative control. Can be overly self-centered or narcissistic.

Psychic: As a psychic number, 1 has leadership quality, there is abundant confidence, with a sense of originality. This can create adverse effects in the form of self-centered attitudes and lack of attention to detail.

Life path: As a life path number, 1 adds a leadership quality that is motivated and self-reliant. Material success is a driving force behind this influence. Personal accomplishment is very important and if not achieved may cause lack of self-worth. When balanced, 1 offers bursts of creative expression and enthusiasm, leading to great original ideas. The energy of 1 thrives when challenged or faced with adversity. This resilience makes for physical and mental strength, along with a fiery determination. The natural leadership skills that accompany the number 1 pairs well with its creative determination, but can cause an unbalanced desire for control.

Innovation and independence play a key role in 1 energy as a life path number. This requires strength and a healthy outlet to vent any creative energy that comes through in abundance. Routines are tough to keep track of and attention to detail can be fleeting at times. Although life path 1 influence can be overly assertive, it is social and, if balanced, can be very welcoming. If left unchecked this energy can lead to narcissism, but overall is friendly and personable. The attraction of peers helps to ease this number's desire for approval, but if left unsatisfied or disapproved of, one may become depressed or lose the confidence that drives to balance this energy.

Being able to listen and follow leads is a lesson to be learned from a life path 1 influence. Being able to follow and be inspired by others is crucial to learning about yourself and the world around you. Letting others take the reins is a great exercise in controlling the need to be bossy or too assertive. Be sure not to let the ego drive all your actions

Name: As a name number, 1 thrives on achieving independence and a leadership role. Innovation and creativity are must-have attributed to attain this goal, although depending on your other numerological influences you may be able to succeed in this venture without originality. Owning a business or other self-employment is comfortable and ideal for name number 1. It is key not to rush to achieve your goals and not to be afraid to accept help along the way.

2 – TWO
Planet: Moon - Color: White - Day: Monday

Psychic: As a psychic number, 2 creates a more sensitive attitude, with more empathy and added social skills. You often may have to do things twice to accomplish them. Number 2 energy may have a more depressive affect, creating anxiety and introverted behavior.

Life Path: As a life path number, 2 influences one to have a sense of peacekeeping and spiritual duty. Listening skills are heightened and empathizing comes easy with this energy. Diplomacy and the ability to diffuse aggressive situations is a very positive quality if the life path 2. When used for a morally upright reason these diplomatic skills can be very useful, but they can also be used for unjust reasons, such as personal gain at the expense of others. Deep thought and intuition are added spiritual qualities of this number. This attracts peers to seek insight and confide in someone with a healthy life path 2 influence.

Living with the life path 2 energy makes for a balanced and idealistic attitude. Being able to see the balance in the most mundane of events helps one to see the interconnectedness of everything around us. This insight into the natural connection of all things allows one to see both sides of the world, positive and negative. Unbiased and fair, life path 2 energy wants the best for everyone; this honest sincerity attracts others to find life path 2 as a mediator for troubling situations. Being open to compromise is a positive quality, but can lead to an unhealthy amount of self-sacrifice which in turn can be detrimental.

Routine and habitual behavior are a must to balance this energy. Maintaining patterns in day to day life helps to organize the balanced perspective but can lead to a lack of adventure and excitement. Focus on work and achievement can add to the chance of being caught up in a routine that takes up too much free time. If routines are broken, life path 2 energy can become anxious. And with such a balanced view of the world, when one wishes to express one's own personal opinion, they often come across overly extreme or zealous. Also with the balanced perspective, it may be difficult to make decisions or choose between two different options. This may lead the life path 2 influence to lead to a lack of competitiveness, leading to lost opportunity and lack of assertion.

Name: As a name number, 2 thrives on finding ways to understand humanity and its spiritual implications. The natural ability to work with others and diffuse conflict is key to attaining these goals. Name number 2 has great potential to be spiritually adept and help others to reach their spiritual goals. Seeking a path in teaching or philosophy is comfortable for these name numbers. Esoteric practices are attractive and magical endeavors come easily. The natural talent of occult studies and spirit work may lend itself to nervousness and anxiety if not balanced.

3 – THREE
Planet: Jupiter - Color: Yellow - Day: Thursday

Psychic: As a psychic number, 3 adds stamina to the equation, with quick mental and physical readiness. Restlessness is a constant quality of 3 energy, making for an expressive quality. An unbalanced amount of this quality may lead to a scattered and unorganized mindset and potential exhaustion.

Life Path: As a life path number, 3 offers an immense amount of creative potential, leading to insight into the expressive faculties and artistic mediums. Well-spoken with excellent communication skills, this energy helps one to be adept in writing, speaking and acting. Optimism is abundant with a bright attitude as life path 3 people are quick to entertain or please others with innovative or improvised gestures. The overly optimistic behavior focuses on the beauty of the world, but this can lead one to ignore the negative side of life, missing or not anticipating adverse scenarios.

Life path 3 people have a natural tendency to value the present moment, going wherever life takes them or 'going with the flow.' This care-free attitude leads to nomadic behavior and lack of fulfillment with the surroundings of any given place. This energy left unbalanced may lead to debt or other money issues, often leaving the future uncertain for the life path 3 person. This uncertainty can be thrilling but also dangerous or unhealthy.

Along with the desire to travel and move about, life path 3 energy loves the human connection and socializes well. This may lead to reliance on others for fulfillment if left unchecked. The combination of not planning for the future while also not being self-reliant can be troubling to the life path 3, but this is a big lesson to be learned. Time alone is needed just as much as social interaction. Although seemingly resilient and optimistic, life path 3 natives are actually quite sensitive. When they receive disapproval or embarrassment in a social setting, they may become depressed, or even dwell in the event for too long. Balancing these ups and downs are key to growing as a life path 3.

This life path number is notorious as trustworthy romantic partners. While very forgiving and loyal, these natives are emotional and attached to their lovers. This may be negative if an ended relationship has hurt the 3, it could lead to unhealthy attachment or longing. The love of life and people makes the life path 3 enjoyable to be around, but they become attached may push peers away leading to loneliness or introverted attitudes.

Name: As a name number, 3 thrives on achieving artistic and creative aptitude. Getting the most out of life and truly embracing the moment. This ability to uplift others through creative endeavors is the key to this name number's influence. Becoming an artist or entertainer is comfortable for name number 3. Other numerological factors may play into the creative outlets to be less about art and more fitting for creative ideas during other lines of work. This name number also aims to acquire lifelong friends and also be a reliable friend themselves. Communication, emotional expression and friendly support are key traits for this name number.

4 – FOUR

Planet: Uranus / Rahu - Color: Gold - Day: Sunday

Psychic: As a psychic number, 4 adds an organized quality, with responsible awareness and discipline. Rationality and practicality are other aspects of 4 energy, although this can limit creativity and emotional expression, it overly influential can lead to stubbornness.

Life Path: As a life path number, 4 is practical and organized, with a knack for constructive actions and hands-on skills. Life path 4 natives are great to trust and calm, building physical things and emotional relationships throughout all of society. This life path offers many talents or 'jack of all trades' skill sets, often leading to ideals that are set on upholding a just perspective.

With a balanced and grounded mindset, life path 4 natives still reach for the stars with their life plans, often conceiving farfetched goals and ideals. This is very motivating but can lead to goals that are not attainable without a lifetime's worth of hard work and dedication. To achieve these big goals the 4 native may come across to others as distracted or stubborn. This one-pointedness could lead the native to miss opportunities or ignore personal affairs in favor of work. This determination is a positive quality, but if you can't stay with your convictions and the job doesn't get completed, the native may feel an overwhelming sense of failure.

If the native can balance out the obsessive need to be constructive, the life path 4 influence can be great for practical perspectives with a sense of perfectionism in day to day life. Taming the need to set farfetched goals and not focus on the biggest picture is a grand lesson to be learned for this life path. If this obsessive behavior is channeled into personal relationships, such as marriage or friendship, the native can be an exceptional companion. Dedicated to their friends and family, the life path 4 energy is dependable and caring, often finding balance in emotional situations, not letting emotions get the best of them.

Name: As a name number, 4 strives to attain a greater sense of order in a chaotic world. Working in service to their fellow man, this name number's energy is practical and logical. Determined to complete tasks that help humanity progress, engineering, medicine and technological fields of work are favorable. If accompanied by other fitting numerological factors, this name number may find a career in music or other artistic medium with emphasis on uplifting work. This number aims to teach that as the constructed and organized builder, they must also give up control at times, acknowledging that they must let loose and 'go with the flow' every once in a while.

5 – FIVE
Planet: Mercury - Color: Green - Day: Wednesday

Psychic: As a psychic number, 5 energy seems to add a sociable and 'team player' attitude. While working well with others is a positive attribute, it could lead to reliance on group atmospheres. With added skills in being analytical, the quick nature of the 5 influence could lead to lack of fulfillment with a steady routine.

Life Path: As a life path number, 5 offers a very forward-thinking perspective, with a desire to move society and culture into more progressive states. This need to be ahead of the game and constantly evolving is driven by the want for freedom. Complex and deep thinking, these natives aim to adventure and learn about the world as much as possible, hoping to gain insight into how the world works. Seeking answers to the toughest questions, exploring the unknown and questioning the status quo.

Life path 5 natives are among the most empathetic of all people, valuing justice and fairness for all people of the world. This desire for freedom leads one to continue moving sporadically in search for answers. This could lead to many incomplete goals and loose ends. Many times, if these natives are unsatisfied if they do not receive answers quickly, leading them to move on to other questions.

This number's energy adds a motivating quality to the native, making them adept in organizing groups, especially progressive political groups or organizations. Working with people is ideal for the native, hoping not to get caught in a mundane routine. If used for morally righteous reasons these skills are very positive but can be corrupted by materialism or greed.

Life path 5 natives don't want to be contained or fenced in. This makes it tough to keep a romantic relationship or career afloat for long periods of time. Trust is very important for the native in any relationship, romantic or platonic. If the native knows they are trusted, they can better navigate the relationship without feeling bogged down or possessed.

The skillful life path 5 native is driven and talented but often lacks one-pointedness, moving from project to project or town to town. This lack of content may lead to self-indulgence and narcissism as a means to gratify the desires to be in control and free.

Name: As a name number, 5 strives to accomplish positive social change, progressing society toward justice and freedom. With a wide array of talents, this name number aims to teach one to adapt well to change. This adaptability is the key to success in initiating social change and learning how to reach out to other people and think quickly when analyzing a situation. Most any field of work benefits from these skills, but without a career or hobby that implements social change, this name number may become unfulfilled or bored with their work. Balancing out over analytical thought and learning to stay focused are key to succeeding in these ways.

6 – SIX

Planet: Venus - Color: Silver / Blue - Day: Friday

Psychic: As a psychic number, 6 has a very nurturing effect, creating natural aptitude toward family affairs and parenting. Honesty and carefulness lend to the 6 energy and its friendly attitude but be cautioned about naivety and a tendency to worry too much.

Life Path: As a life path number, 6 offers nurturing and domestic skills, giving insight to the native about parenting and caring for others. Whether it's family or other acquaintances these natives are typically leaders in truth and fairness. The instinctual nature to provide and balance the surroundings offers an abundance of love and kindness for the life path 6 natives. Community affairs and other political things are heavy on the minds of these natives. This number is stern in its beliefs and holds firm its need for truth and honesty.

The supportive nature of life path 6 natives makes the problems of humanitarianism and domestic affairs easily solvable. Being inherently adept at helping others and sympathizing with them allows these natives the skills to take on the burdens of others. This may lead to 'biting off more than they can chew' and misjudging the amount of emotional baggage they carry. If left unbalanced this can have detrimental effects in the future. Feeling obligated to take on other's problems and responsibilities can easily become a problem of authoritarian concern as well. Life path 6 natives should take great care to not uptake too many burdens and to not use their caring nature to take control of every situation.

With this sense of obligatory service to society, life path 6 natives are often considered selfless and caring romantic partners, as well as being a supportive member of the immediate family and community. Quick to lend a hand or financial support, this number's attitude towards material possessions is charitable. Life path 6 natives can maintain a balanced life by staying true to their convictions and not letting their natural empathetic state to become exhausting.

Name: As a name number, 6 strives to adopt an incredible sense of love and compassion towards others. Offering comfort for others, nurturing a family and charitable contributions are natural energies that accompany this name number. Working in the non-profit sector, teaching and medical fields are comfortable career paths for this number. Focus on the community is key in this number's efforts, offering empathy towards the less fortunate and reaching out to assist those in need. The lesson that name number 6 aims to teach is to learn to be selfless and balanced when helping others, rather than proud or self-righteous.

7 – SEVEN
Planet: Neptune / Ketu - Color: Blue / White - Day: Monday

Psychic: As a psychic number, 7 adds more attention to detail, with a sense of originality. 7 is insightful and mindful, with added skills in foresight and improvisation. As a natural loner quality, this energy opposes authority and tends to contribute a stubborn attitude.

Life Path: As a life path number, 7 natives are equipped with exceptional observation skills, with a tendency toward critically analyzing most situations. Quick thinking and a good judge of character, life path 7 natives are naturally able to evaluate situations and make accurate assessments. This number's attitude is filled with high expectations, consistently upholding a standard of living and working that is above the status quo. These keen observation skills are accompanied by a peaceful attitude towards others.

Life path 7 natives are sociable but reserved and on guard during social interaction. Typically, 'sizing up' the situation before letting their guard down, this number uses its over-analytical mindset to detect false friends and have the foresight to prepare for unfavorable occurrences. Once these life path 7 natives get to know someone and ensure they are trustworthy, they open up and easily develop friendships that are long-lasting. These high standards for companionship make group situations and organizations unattractive to these natives.

The lonesome attitude of life path 7 natives inspires an introspective thought process. Time spent away from urban areas and in nature are valuable occasions for them to work out some intellectual awareness of society. This may lead to loneliness and social anxiety if left unbalanced. One key lesson of life path 7 natives is to learn how to take their deep and intellectual thoughts and use them to contribute to society. In many cultures, 7 is a spiritual or magically significant number. This inherent spiritual awareness is a positive attribute if used with morally upright intentions. Otherwise, the temptation to use their natural skills for selfish reasons can be the downfall of these natives. Some may experience an overstimulation of ego when they realize their potential; this can lead to constant inner conflict as well as difficulty remaining in relationships with others.

Name: As a name number, 7 strives to find universal truths through analytical thought and spiritual endeavor. Whether scientific truths or esoteric truths, name number 7 seeks vigorously the unknown and pure. Introspective and secluded this number influences one to distance themselves from others in exchange for deep thought and in-depth studies. Teaching, spiritual work and sciences are favorable paths to walk with this number's energy. Although peaceful and calm, this number may lead to loneliness and lack of compassion for others, the main lesson taught by this number is the power of truth and the sacrifice one needs to make to find it.

8 – EIGHT
Planet: Saturn - Color: Black / Purple - Day: Saturday

Psychic: As a psychic number, 8 lends a skillful business mindset, adding balanced judgement and reliability. This responsible number is trustworthy and supports a just cause. There is an added adverse effect of materialism and a tendency to be controlling.

Life Path: As a life path number, 8 has an organizational influence; this is complemented by natural skills to govern any situation. Life path 8 natives have an immense amount of ambitious fervor. Motivated by earthly knowledge and material gain, this ambition often manifests as big ideas and hard to reach goals. Luckily this number's energy is also notorious for rigid and hard working, always completing the task at hand.

With a life path number of 8, many people have a natural knack to read a room and gain insight about their peers by observing and judging. This allows the native to easier manipulate and manage their environment and those in it. This ability ensures that the objective at hand is completed, although if abused, this ability can cause great harm to others or even lead to an unhealthy habit to manipulate for selfish reasons. Manipulation and desire for material gain can be a perilous combination, leading to a greedy and power-hungry behavior.

As long as materialism doesn't get in the way, life path 8 natives can be reliable and supportive companions. It is a true lesson to these natives to learn to balance family and friends with work. Being financially supportive goes a long way, but learning to be emotionally supportive and loving is the key to balancing the workaholic mindset of life path 8 natives. The overwhelming desire to succeed in the workforce can lead to detachment from emotions and an inability to express the emotions.

Name: As a name number, 8 strives to achieve success through material gain, seeking advancement in the 'real world.' This number requires a steady income and plenty of assurance of material availability. The drive and ambition of this number adds a great quality to any line of work, reliable and consistent one may own or operate a business or make their way up the corporate ladder. Hard work and good judgement help reach these goals, but the ultimate lesson of this number's influence is to balance out material wealth and emotional wealth. It is important to not value money and power over love and truth.

9 - NINE
Planet: Mars - Color: Red - Day: Tuesday

Psychic: As a psychic number, 9 influences one's natural energy to be driven, with a tendency to use that drive to tackle humanitarian issues. Open minded and empathetic. The number 9's influence is emotionally motivated and generous. An unbalanced amount of this energy can lead to exhaustion and attachment.

Life Path: As a life path number, 9 has a generous spirit that is charitable and set on changing the world for the better. These natives are reliable and live up to their proud attitudes by living with honor. Their perspectives are unbiased and fair, paying close attention to avoid prejudice of hateful behavior. Empathy for the underprivileged lends a compassionate attitude to these natives. They are often prone to charitable works and community outreach. Number 9 life path natives are often considered to have an obligatory duty to better mankind; if this desire is left unfulfilled the person may feel unimportant or unsatisfied with how their lives turned out. This is a very high standard, but even being a positive influence on one person will better mankind, so be open-minded about this attribute.

The charitable nature of life path number 9 natives often leads to a selfless nature that does not value material possessions. This lack of materialism may cause one to be too frivolous with their financial situation, which in turn could lead to unhealthy means of sustaining oneself. While this selfless perspective is a positive quality, it is recommended that these natives learn to balance their charitable nature with self-reliance and financial stability.

Life path 9 natives have an unmistakably heavy presence. Their ability to steal the attention out of a room makes them very attractive as a companion. The open-minded and selfless attitude makes for a welcoming atmosphere, friendships are abundant and the native is attentive and caring with their peers. Within these relationships, this number has an influence that keeps the native sensitive to misunderstandings and disapproval. The native needs companionship that does not rely on materialism to be fulfilling.

This sensitive nature is also a great inspiration for artistic expression. Having such an inherent compassion towards others and the world leaves the native bursting with emotion, an artistic outlet is very beneficial for the native. Philosophy, painting, acting and music are all common hobbies among life path 9 natives. Competitive fields like office work and sales are not the most favorable for this number's energy. This life path may seem to be more challenging than the others, but this is the lesson of this path in itself, humanitarian challenges and sacrifice.

Name: As a name number, 9 strives to understand humanity and learn compassion. This nurturing energy aims to create an understanding, inspirational attitude while working well with others. Medicine, law, politics and spiritual fields of work are favorable for this number. Relationships, both romantic and platonic, are very important for this name number. Being nurturing and caring for friends and family are key to success for name number 9. The lesson of this influence is a lesson in understanding, to learn to cherish humanity and to teach unconditional love.

An Added note about the number nine:

The number 9 is a very distinct number. Unlike the other numbers it does not have an opposite; it stands alone in nature and feels dutiful as the highest number before the numbers repeat themselves. 9 is often considered the 'last' or final number so is attributed with completion and spiritual growth. Some systems believe that is 9 is your life path number then you are in a final evolutionary stage and may discover valuable esoteric truths if you spend your time wisely.

We also see a curious pattern in number 9 calculations. As you practice these calculations, you will realize that any number added to 9 is reduced to itself. For example, 2+9=11, 1+1=2. This is consistent infinitely and allows us to cancel out 9s during calculations. 9 may as well be zero when we are calculating, and yet it still holds influence if found in our numerology. Here's another example:

Birthday: 11/29/1989

1+1+2+9+1+9+8+9=40

4+0=4

4 is the life path number

Now let's cancel the nines.

1+1+2+~~9~~+1+~~9~~+8+~~9~~

1+1+2+1+8=13

1+3=4

We find that this as a useful shortcut when calculating these numbers; this also gives 9 a curious nature that stands out from the crowd. In Vedic astrology, number squares are used to find shapes and patterns in the nine base numbers. A box that is 9 by 9 is drawn up and multiplied to fill the table. Then the numbers are reduced to single digits. If you were to connect all of one number you will see a shape. Opposite numbers have the same shapes only mirrored to each other; 9 does not have a mirrored shape and actually doesn't have a symmetrical shape at all. This is very curious and should be contemplated upon, learning the number 9 nature is very important to see the interconnectedness of all the other numbers.

Now we have a solid reference for some of the more important calculations to use when practicing numerology. These attributes and definitions are meant to be a loose guide; no one type of lifestyle is going to fit every person with a '2' life path number. These attributes are simply the natural make-up of the subtle influence of numbers. Environment, astrology and religious belief systems change these natural influences to create the complex energetic being that we are. These subtle influences are tough to track, but our goals here are to better ourselves and our lives, not solve the mysteries of the universe. Use your numerology to your liking, experiment and see what parallels you see in yourself and in the world around you.

With these three main calculations in mind, let's look at some other calculations that are more or less specific to personal lives and more broadly calculated for success or protection. We will also look at notorious numbers from many cultures and see how they have become famous as omens or good luck.

CHAPTER 3
Success Numbers And Practice

The universe of number is infinite. Therefore, many other calculations can be made to balance and make good use of your numerology. The three calculations used above are excellent for getting insight into your personal natural makeup, but other numbers hold a more general influence over everyday life. These numbers can vary from culture to culture and change over time, but let's discuss some other ways to calculate for specific reasons and other notable numbers and their personalities.

With these numbers, as well as the main three above, you can work with them to achieve your desires and time your plans to be on favorable days. Some dedicated numerologists have mastered the art of forecasting, being able to anticipate major life events and even manipulate them. These practices go hand in hand with astrology, but more on that later.

Numbers for prosperity

Many people find their way to numerology in search of assistance with monetary gain. Everyone could use a little more money in their pocket and numerology can help. Once you've learned your personal numerology choose a favorable line of work that suits your natural make-up. Also planning certain events, such as job interviews or job-hunting days, on favorable days will assist you in gaining consistent income.

It is good to keep in mind there is no 'get rich quick' scheme to be done with numerology. While working with these numbers will increase the probability of you receiving your desired outcome, if the odds are against you in a great way you may not see immediate results. The lottery is a good example. If you have a 1 in 1,000,000 chance to win and your work with numerology lessens that to 1 in 900,000 chance it still has been successful numerological work, but you would never know and the chances are still stacked against you. Choose wisely how you spend your time and focus on finding ways to generate income since a nice job is more likely that 1 million dollars falling into your lap. Be creative and specific in your workings.

1

1 is a great number to work with if you are seeking prosperity. This number is thought to be key in achieving success, consider the ideas of being number one in a ranking system or being the first to do something. Choosing 1, 10, 19 or 28 as days to start new jobs or searching for jobs is recommended.

The number 1 may also be used to start new ventures or transition into a better position in the job you already have. Start new projects on these dates and anticipate these dates as days of change and growth.
Working with the sun as a symbolic version of 1 is helpful as well. Sundays that are 1, 10, 19 or 28 dates are especially potent for 1 energy. Offerings can be left to the sun in the form of water, incense and of course, money. This work is especially potent and should be handled with respect and humility.

2

The number two is thought to be unfavorable for financial gain. The 2 energy often delays things, often having to attempt things twice to succeed. While the numbers 11 and 22 are known for abundance, this could be elusive for money. It is recommended that job searching and asking for raises should not be done on day 2, 11, 20 and 29.

3

The number 3 can be tricky to work with for prosperity purposes. Although known for acquiring wealth, it is often emotional or loving wealth, rather than money. If 3 is heavy in your numerology, it will require intense focus to gain and maintain monetary wealth. Spontaneous spending should be avoided.

4

If you have trouble keeping jobs, 4 may be able to help, but this number requires discipline and hard work. If you work with your hands, 4 can help you maintain your job and acquire raises. Investing time and hard work goes well with the dates 4, 8, 13, 22, 31.

5

The number five works well with financial situations, a dedicated career benefits from the 5 energy, but savings and investments are a must if you have heavy 5 energy in your personal numerology. Days 5, 14 and 23 are excellent days to seek investment opportunities and open bank accounts.

6

The number 6 works well for abundant prosperity; this influence is very prominent later in life. Working with six to prepare for retirement or save money for big adventures is recommended. Days 6, 15 and 24 are great days to take care of debts and plan future finances.

7

The number 7 can go either way with financial situations. Financial challenges and significant financial gains are common with heavy 7 influence. This is risky to work with for prosperity so isn't generally recommended unless it places well with other numerological or astrological factors.

8

The number 8 is great for prosperity; this number is so organized and driven towards financial gain that it is almost unavoidable if you want to be materially wealthy. Logical and calm days 8, 17 and 26 are great for hard working days and finishing projects. 8 energy is necessary to complete tasks in a timely manner so pairs well with the 2 energy, 8+2=10, 1+0=1, and so you also get the 1 energy from these workings.

8 may cause some troubles along the way in the form of deadlines and disrupted timelines. Saturn is the planetary ruler of 8 and dictates time and logic. Working with Saturn can be risky so approach at your own risk with offerings or ritual workings.

9

The number 9 energy attracts prosperity constantly, but the influence also creates a lack of material desire. This can be good for acquiring small sums of money quickly but will be spent immediately. The unique features of 9 will allow you to gain money, but it will have to be with the intention of using the money for selfless reasons, such as charitable works and humanitarian change.

Numbers for love

For relationships and love numerology we will be predominantly be using life path numbers, but these numbers can be worked with on their own as well to find compatibility and balanced relationships, platonic or romantic.

Some systems of numerology find that if two people share a life path number that they are compatible as having much in common, but may not find growth within the relationship. Numbers that are opposites may have differing viewpoints, but the opposite opinions offer room for growth and stimulating conversation.

While many numbers can be compatible with a wide array of different number combinations, we will discuss the attributes of each life path number as a lover and friend below.

1

In relationships, this number loves to be in charge. Being straightforward and self-reliant is key to this number's compatibility. The need to be in control can lead to self-conscious behavior if they feel like things are out of their control. Creative activities and exercises are a must and consistency are needed.

2

In relationships, the number two really enjoys being a couple. Sharing responsibilities and living as much of their lives as possible with their companions is an ultimate goal. As a romantic partner, this number is sensitive but also empathetic in a great way. Constant affection and teamwork are key.

3

In relationships, life path number 3 natives may seem casual and not invested, but deep down they're very kind and caring. Socializing and hosting gatherings is one way that this number shows its affection. As a romantic partner, the outer shell may need to be cracked to get their reciprocated affection.

4

In relationships, this number is devoted and strong. Being able to uplift their companions, the life path 4 natives are nurturing and attentive. Material gain and emotional balance are key to this number's personal life. Spontaneity and adventures are great since this number is so reliable and enjoyable to be around.

5

Communication is key for relations with life path 5 natives. Their conversation is witty and original and they expect the same from their partners. Physical appearances need to be distinct and socializing is needed to please this number's desire to stimulate all the senses. Going out to eat or to concerts is a great way to please the number 5

6

The number 6 has long been associated with beauty and sex. Venus is the ruling planet for this number and it shows. As a companion this number loves to be responsible for its family and friends, cleaning, cooking and all around caring for the day to day tasks needed to keep a home. These partners are quick to empathize and love fixing a bad day or adverse scenario.

7

For relationships, life path 7 is mysterious and powerful. Intellectual or spiritual conversation is very important, as well as adventures to meaningful places, like ruins or mountains. With magical tendencies, these companions may seek universal truths and expect your assistance, be prepared for intense, out of this world energy.

8

As we learned in the prosperity section, 8 is a great number for logic and money. These things come through in relationships as well. Balance and strength give this number a very attractive quality for those seeking foundation and security. Material goals and adventures abound as you spend time with these natives, they typically love to brag about their lovers and friends.

9

This number has an 'old soul' mentality when it comes to relationships. Deep, insightful conversations and mental clarity is key to pleasing the number 9. Having a compassionate attitude toward humanity is also very important; charitable work and volunteering is a huge part of this number's life. Showing immense love for their partners and the whole world, this unique number is unforgettable as a companion.

Motivational numbers

These numbers are relatively new in the numerology sphere. It is calculated by finding the value of only the vowels in your full name and then reducing that number to a single digit if it isn't already one. This number reveals hidden emotions and desires, thus motivating one to aspire toward these desires. Fears may be revealed or even other obstacles that may be secretly hindering you from achieving what you want. Contemplation on these numbers is very therapeutic for confidence and mental clarity.

Let's take a look at the individual numbers and what they may be hiding about your true self. This revealing calculation may be eye-opening too many, but keep in mind that you may have unhealthy desires and well as balanced ones. Be aware of which is which.

1

Motivational number 1 reveals your desire to be the center of attention. You wish to be a leader and feel that you have the best answers. You are content as long as you are in control of any given situation. You secretly wish you could work alone since you have the best ideas. A desire to be the first to accomplish something or be number one on a competitive list is common. This can manifest into narcissism and lack of empathy if left unchecked.

2

Motivational number two reveals to you that you desperately need peace in your day to day life. The less the change and drama, the better. The basic necessities and a small circle of loved ones are all it takes to motivate you. You wish to have a significant other that can be the hub of your life. Harmony and routine are ideal, and adventure is not favored.

3

The motivational number 3 desires fame and glamour, with emphasis on entertaining others. Your popularity is important to you and you gauge your success on how well-liked you are. Home décor and appearances need to be fashionable and contemporary. The desire for constant attention and interaction with others is constant, as well as wanting to spread creative ideas and share yourself with others.

4

Deep down, the motivational number 4 wants everything to be structured and logical. If each detail of your life could be meticulously planned, then you would do it. Material structure and organization are desired at all times. You feel it is your responsibility to build a balanced home and environment. Practicality is a motivating force that is unavoidable.

5

The motivational number five desperately needs freedom and change. Having the freedom you want will allow you to cater to other needs such as adventure and experiences that are not mundane. Stimulation of the five senses is required constantly and may become obsessive. Making new friends and lovers is a common desire as well

6

As a motivational number, 6 reveals your desire to create a harmonious life. You value fairness and can't stand injustice. You wish to teach others and help as many people as possible if you can't contribute in helpful ways, then you are unfulfilled. You have a fiery need to create and be expressive throughout day to day life.

7

Motivational number 7 imparts an intense desire to be alone. Quiet meditation and studying are ideal ways to spend your free time; without this much needed alone time, you may be restless and scatterbrained. Privacy is needed to achieve these goals, and deep down you may want to be alone the majority of the time. Communication through intelligible conversation is necessary. Retreats into nature for indefinite amount of time are fitting

8

Motivational number 8 reveals a hungry need for material gain and power. This attitude can easily become uncontrollable; you may feel like you would do anything to achieve authority or riches. You want to own all the latest technology, buy nice cars and overall really show off your wealth. You wish to tell others what to do, boasting your material success to prove that your way is best.

9

You have an undying desire to broaden your spiritual capabilities and learn about the true nature of reality. You desperately want others to join you on your spiritual quests and humanitarian endeavors. Your emotions get the best of you since you feel so strongly toward the entire universe; this can be tough to balance at times. Practicality alludes you as you think with your emotions, chasing idealistic goals rather than material ones.

Personal growth numbers

11 and 22

These numbers hold a distinct energy that we need to discuss briefly. These numbers are considered 'master numbers.' This is in reference to the fact that these numbers are more adept at spiritual conquest. Added awareness and powers of perception are endowed with the influence of these numbers. Many who have these numbers as life path numbers often feel strange or have run-ins with the paranormal. This may lead one to think they have a problem but, in fact, they are more conscious of other worlds and various other intelligence.

If these added powers of the spiritual nature are ignored, there may be consequences that cannot be reversed. This is a huge responsibility that is owed to the individual and humanity as a whole. Some use these powers for evil purposes to gain selfish desires; this should be avoided as well. With added pressure to be a cosmic hero to humanity, these numbers as life path numbers should be handled with care. It is recommended to seek out a spiritual teacher if these numbers are heavy in your numerology.

CHAPTER 4
Astrology

The ancient art of astrology has been practiced since before history. The oldest known ancient ruins that have been discovered show evidence that the humans there were using the stars to better understand the world and navigate the human experience. The stars were used for calendrical timing, spiritual magic, personal empowerment and divination. All ancient cultures have astrology at the core of their religions and spiritual practices.

These elaborate astrological systems have been discovered in India, China and South America to only name a few. Reliance on the stars was necessary for everyday life in ancient times, today we see less emphasis in the symbolic and spiritual nature of the stars and planets, and more focus on scientific function and space travel. This creates a huge gap in the human experience that needs to be filled. Let's learn the basics and return to our home in the stars.

What is astrology?

Astrology is an ancient practice that boasts powerful secrets to magic, spirituality and the origins of humanity. By studying celestial events, humans have seen that the heavens mirror events on earth. Since this is the case the Hermetic idiom 'as above, so below' is fitting. The personalities and behavior of the planets go hand in hand with numerological approaches to personal empowerment and the nature of reality. While there is no way to scientifically tell how astrology works, we see that many people have had success with this complex system, from early man to modern day astrologers.

It is thought that the position of the planets at the moment you are born offers symbolic insight into your personality and major life events that will take place. This natal chart is your natural cosmic make-up and can be used to take control of your life and its lessons. While these natal charts are often accurate, we need to also consider other circumstances that affect our personalities, such as religion and upbringing.

Learning personal qualities is one perk of astrology, but also the timing is a huge factor to consider. Before technology and other calendars imposed by the Catholic Church, humanity used the heavens as its calendar. By studying your natal chart, you may be able to better time major life events or big occasions like weddings or speeches. This astrologically timed lifestyle is one of the major keys to unlocking the power of astrology. This is the most practical way to use astrology and it not alter your worldview or be overly self-involved. Personality traits aside, astrology has a lot to offer in the way of perspective and empowerment.

Ancient maps of the zodiac show the constellations and planets that are easily observed with the naked eye. These constellations have ancient glyphs and earthly symbolism to help humans retain the information for thousands of years. As these planets move in front of various constellations, they impart a combination of their own energy and that of the constellation they are housed in. This can offer any number of results, in fact being so complex to potentially house all of human experience in one symbolic map.

Before telescopes, the human eye could not see any planets past Saturn. This is quite a small universe compared to the infinitely expanding one we have today, but modern astrology still mainly focuses on our solar system and the effects of the closest planets and stars. This complex offers immense potential to grow spiritually and personally with just a small amount of studying, and yet is complex enough to take entire lifetimes to perfect and master.

Historical significance

Astrology is scientifically dated to have been around since the 2nd millennium BCE, but it is safe to say that it was practiced before then. Whether it was timing harvest season, empowering leaders or predicting major disasters, astrology was a foundational science of the ancient world. It was taken very seriously and used to great success by people who had the resources and intellect to use it. Celestial events were viewed as meaningful signs of impending abundance or trouble. Imagine seeing a full eclipse in ancient times; this is menacing enough as it is even in our modern era.

Evidence shows ancient humans have been searching for meaning in the skies for as far back as we can document. Cave paintings and bone carvings show evidence of human's attempts to record and make sense of their relationship with the night sky. As far back as 20,000 years, evidence has shown documentation of moon cycles and eclipses. With the advent of agriculture farmers used rising constellations to know when to plant seeds and when harvest time was nearing. Temples are constructed to align with these heavenly signs; the pyramids at Giza are the most popular example of this.

Mesopotamian evidence is thought to be the earliest record of astrology, and curiously mirrors Hellenistic astrology of Greece and Rome. These systems both use the zodiac, trine aspects, planetary rulers and dividing the heavens into twelve houses. This is strange for two systems from different continents to use similar techniques.

Astrology sees its lineage form and change with the times and cultures it influenced. These cultures share ideas and practices and form powerful systems of astrological workings that still are used today. Evidence shows the astrological techniques traveling the ancient world. Documents in China during the Zhou dynasty show that complex systems were used for centuries. Egyptian and Babylonian astrological techniques were adopted by Alexandria, being similar to today's horoscope astrology. Ancient Greece and Rome found great insight into Asian astrology as the cultures mixed during Alexander the Great's conquests. The Greek and Roman Hellenistic astrology is familiar as the planets are given the names of gods and goddesses commonly found in the history books and mythology.

Many Roman philosophers denied the validity of astrology; this skepticism is found in the powerful Christian church as well. Christianity denounced astrological practices, although the Bible is filled with star lore and symbolism. Soon the scientific study of the heavens was deemed astronomy and valid, while astrology was considered useless and to be the art of demons. The Renaissance saw a short rise in astrological popularity only to be snuffed out by the Enlightenment period. The 19th century saw a rise in the practice of astrology, mainly personality horoscopes.

Up until the past few hundreds of years, astrological themes were found in almost every aspect of life. Literature, music, painting and even science were rooted in astrological inspiration and symbolism. Astrology was considered scholarly and of the utmost importance to the progression of humanity. This cannot be ignored as the great artists and thinkers who set the foundation of our modern era relied heavily on astrology to reach the heights that they did in their fields of work. This was no simple fad, these influential people were working with the planets and their energies to create powerful art and literature, instilling within their work the very nature of the planets themselves.

The long history of astrology is rooted in mystery and ancient wisdom lost to science and laboratory testing. While this art has history on its side, science is in no rush to try and prove the complex theories about astrology. Dedicated astrologers have found great success in their personal lives and have also opted to go into a career as astrologers to help others who don't have the time to work out the complexities on their own. Today there is a revival of astrology and many other occult studies. With social media and the internet, it may be tough to filter out true astrologers versus con artists. But at the same time, we have more and more people openly admitting their success with astrology and its powerful effects on all of our lives.

Below we will explore these themes and focus on common keywords that are specific to astrology. We will go over vocabulary, natal charts and practices to help you better understand how this art is related to numerology.

Natal charts

If you could somehow take a snapshot of the planet's positions at the moment of your birth, you would have your natal alignments. This chart is circular and divided into twelve sections with significant celestial objects placed at the exact degree they were located when you were born. These charts are difficult to calculate without a computer, but it can be done. For beginners, it is recommended to go online or use an app to calculate and view your natal chart.

You will need to know your birth date, time of birth and location of birth to have the most accurately calculated chart. If you do not know your time of birth, the position of fast-moving inner planets may be off by a degree or two.

By having access to your natal chart, you can study your personal astrology and learn what your natural celestial make-up consists of. Memorizing and keeping track of your transits and alignments will improve your astrological practice greatly, allowing you to anticipate major life events or major events on favorable days.

The placement of the planets in your natal chart dictates what kind of influence you are exposed to at any given time. The Planets will be in a zodiac sign and then also in one of the twelve houses.

Planets

The planets are the closest celestial bodies to the earth. When we reference planets, please keep in mind, this includes the sun and earth's moon, although they are not technically planets. These planets all have a certain personality that influences us depending on their placement in our natal chart. The planets keep moving, of course, but our natal placement is unchanged. This means that when planets make a full trip through the zodiac, they are back at their original placement in your chart, this is called a transit. Different planets take more time to complete their trip through the zodiac depending on how far away from the sun they are. The trip through the entire zodiac is synonymous with one revolution around the sun.

Before our advanced technology humans would have to watch the skies closely and consistently, astrology is studied from the perspective of Earth. Therefore it is good at the time to not imagine the planets going around the sun, but to view it from our actual perspective. Since the earth is also moving, we see a delicate and complex dance in the heavens where the planets may align from our point of view, or they will appear to move backward in the night sky; this is labeled as the planet being in retrograde.

The constant movement and intricate patterns presented in the heavens is truly incredible. You see the interconnectedness of the planets right there in the sky, and learning the nature of all the planets relationships is important, but starting out it is good to learn how the sun, moon and ascending sign play out in your natal chart. These are among the most influential planets in any chart. As you progress you will learn the personalities of all the planets, keep in mind the closer the planet the more obvious the influence is. This is why the moon and sun are so important, they appear the closest in our solar system and also quite literally sustain life on earth.

The planets in your chart make-up your natural astrological make-up, these influences are powerful and if treated wisely can be manipulated to improve your life or forecast the future. Many other factors play a huge role in your overall personality and life, but for our purposes here we will give a general description of the planets and their personalities. How these energies behave and which parts of your life they affect will depend on what sign they are in and what house they are in.

Sun

The sun is the closest star to our planet. Although it is the hub of our solar system, from our perspective on earth, it appears to be moving across the sky and through the signs of the zodiac. The sun is representative of the ego and the internal essence that is you. This essence is unchanging, a consistent force that energizes your being, dictating decision making and overall ability to control your will power. The sun is symbolic of the will, but what you use your willpower to do is dictated by other planets and their placements. Where the sun placed in your natal chart is a broad overview of who you are, view it as a foundation, one that is to be built upon by the influences of other planets. This is the core of your celestial make-up; your overall demeanor and attitude are governed by this star.

The sun's influence is crucial to understand for beginners learning astrology. It is the power source that allows the other planets to thrive and further influence your life. Study your sun sign and the house it is in and be sure to be aware of its influence throughout the year as it travels through each sign. The sun takes 365 days to go through the entire zodiac; our current calendar is a sun calendar respectively.

Day: Sunday
Number: 1
Exalted: Aries

Moon

The earth's moon is the closest celestial body to the earth. It controls the tides and other physical events on earth. The moon is seen as equally important as the sun in a natal chart, these two are the easiest to follow from earth's perspective, and their teamwork in the sky to welcome night and day is some of the oldest known astrological practices, influencing agriculture, timekeeping and even religion.

In a natal chart, the moon acts as a mirror. Its placement gives insight into how you see yourself in day to day life. Your emotions and instincts are greatly affected by the moon's position. Unconscious patterns that you may not see in yourself can be revealed by working with the moon. The moon's behavior is very fluid; this manifests in some people as erratic mood swings or fleeting emotions that come and go. Regrets and wrongdoings are often caused by unbalanced moon transits or placements. How you decide to be supportive or nurturing to others is governed by the sign that the moon is in. The behaviors influenced by the moon are often not easy to spot unless you know yourself well, or if others know you well or live with you. The little joys in life and spontaneous, sensual pleasures are influenced by the moon; this spontaneity is fitting as the moon travels quickly through the signs of the zodiac, completing its cycle in around 29 days.

The moon is often associated with fertility and feminine energy. The relationship with mothers and other women are often indicative of the moon's influence. These female relationships are often the platonic needs rather than desires that the moon influences. The house the moon positioned in will influence domestic livelihood and what areas of life you are most emotional about.

The moon's cycle is worth noting as well. We can easily see the moon waxing and waning across the night sky. This cycle has an influence as well, the new moon being where the moon is completely dark, is great for planning and new beginnings, whereas the full moon is all about completion and celebration.

Day: Monday
Number: 2
Exalted: Taurus

Jupiter

The planet Jupiter is one of prosperity and optimistic outlook. This planet is the planet of earthly success, often attributed to the wealth of kings and leaders. This joyous planet is the largest in our solar system and acts as such, with a commanding behavior that aims to bring luck and generous gifts if placed favorably in your chart or transiting in a favorable manner. Knowledge, self-assurance and charitable attitudes are manifestations of Jupiter's influence. Philosophy and psychological adeptness is offered by Jupiter to those who are friends of the planet; this leads those who are in line with Jupiter to be successful in searching for truth and higher education. Idealistic and hard-working, this energy is often a good place to look to improve oneself. Ethics and religious conviction are staples of Jupiter's energy as he smiles upon his natives.

Jupiter's journey through the zodiac takes twelve years to complete; this slow-moving nature manifests as having to work smarter not harder to achieve the optimistic and benevolent attitude that Jupiter symbolizes. Be sure not to become too self-righteous or superficial when working with this gas giant.

Day: Thursday
Number: 3
Exalted: Cancer

Uranus / Rahu
The planet Uranus was the first planet to be discovered using a telescope, this came at a time of disrupting revolution, which is fitting for Uranus and its disruptive behavior. Uranus brings about change, not only for individuals but for whole societies. Uranus is often manifesting in your unconscious, waiting for you to use its energy to discover your true self. This may manifest in a personal epiphany or revelation. New ideas and technologies are the

territories of Uranus as well. We see Uranus placed in distinct houses and signs when major world events happen. Shocking and sudden Uranus stands out as original and uncompromising in its ability to disrupt and harbor dramatic change.

Uranus may disrupt life suddenly and unexpectedly, but the planet moves rather slow, taking 84 years to complete its journey through the zodiac. This lengthy amount of time manifests itself in dramatic transits, when exalted we see Uranus bring dramatic change for entire countries and cultures.

Day: Sunday (Vedic)
Number: 4
Exalted: Scorpio

Mercury
The planet mercury governs travel and communication. Intelligence is also a manifestation of this quick moving little planet. Reasoning is balanced by a favorable mercury placement or transit. How you understand the world around you and your perception of it are qualities that mercury dictates as well. Not unlike a toddler, mercury is quick and curious, often tricky and eager to experience life. Being witty and able to convince others of your perceptive opinion is another manifestation of mercurial energy. There may be a tendency toward restlessness and desire to argue if mercury is transiting unfavorably

Mercury moves quickly through the zodiac signs, taking only one year to complete. Mercury is also notorious for its troublesome retrograde activity. Mercury may go into retrograde 2-3 times a year and these short periods typically bring about trickster occurrences. Travel trouble, miscommunication and important lost items are common themes during Mercury in retrograde. Keeping tracks of these times and preparing for them is recommended, it is not wise to make plans or travel during Mercury in retrograde.

Day: Wednesday
Number: 5
Exalted: Virgo

Venus

The planet Venus is symbolic of love and beauty. This planet its placement influences one's ability to be compassionate and affectionate in a loving way. Often this is mistaken for being only sexual, but in reality, Venus dictates your ability to be loving in almost any area of life, platonic or romantic. People and things you are attracted to or attract are indicative of this planet's influence. Any aspect of attraction, whether its people, music, religion or material things, these are the actions of Venus. Sex appeal and sexual preference are also influenced by this planet, your desires and sexual prowess are greatly influenced by Venus, but sex is a very complicated thing, so the other planets play an important role as well.

Anything that amuses you, preferred social settings and entertainment are the territory of Venus as well. How and why you choose certain friends and hobbies can be representative of Venus's influence as well. This also influences how money is spent. How you express yourself within relationships and whether or not you can maintain balance within them, depending on your gender this may be influenced in different ways. Some systems claim that if you are female, then you use Venus's influence to attract lovers, but if you're male, you use the influence to consider what kind of woman attracts you. Venus is quite close to the sun, where your sun is placed in your chart, Venus will be in the same sign or one of the connecting signs. Be careful with the energy of Venus to not be too overindulgent or envious.

Day: Friday
Number: 6
Exalted: Pisces

Neptune / Ketu

The planet Neptune is responsible for dissolving boundaries. Imagine its discovery; just when humanity was certain about the expanse of our solar system, we find another planet even further away; this dissolved the boundary humans had assumed existed. Neptune has a very watery nature, adhering to containment, but also breaking the walls of its container. Neptune is symbolic of other realms, such as the underworld, or deep oceanic caverns.

Just when you think you may know something Neptune will change the rules, or dissolve your patterns of thinking. Hallucinatory and elusive, this planet will bring visions and insights into other dimensions that humans cannot see. This may also bring about confusion and fogginess depending on your relationship with the planet.

Neptune's journey through the zodiac takes around 165 years, contemplating this long amount of time and visualizing the path is an otherworldly experience. Mystical and intense this planet's energy may drive one to madness with intense vision and spiritual fervor. Escapism and fantastical notions manifest readily with an unfavorable Neptune placement. Drug use, dreaming, addiction and false idolization all are supported by Neptune. But also performance, acting and dance are inspired by this planet's dimension defying behavior. Try to stay grounded when working with Neptune and don't let the fantastic visions lure you into insanity.

Day: Monday
Number: 7
Exalted: Leo

Saturn
The planet Saturn is the farthest planet away from the earth that can be seen with the naked eye. Often considered a negative planet, this is misleading since all planets have their balance of good vs. evil. Still, Saturn is malefic and often governs negative situations such as death, unfortunate events and disapproval. Saturn keeps all the other planets in check by imposing boundaries and restrictions. Saturn ensures that Venus isn't too lustful, or that Mars isn't overly violent. Saturn is the father of the solar system, dictating time, and therefore, governing life and death itself.

Saturn treads lightly, taking almost thirty years to complete his zodiac journey. This thirty-year anniversary manifests itself as mid-life crisis, often called the 'Saturn return' approaching the thirtieth birthday is a time of transformation for every human, for better or worse. Laws, delays, safety and solid practical structure are the gifts Saturn brings to an otherwise chaotic world.

Completion of important projects and endings, in general, are supported by Saturn.

Often morose and cold, the old man is a symbolic representation of Saturn in many paintings and images of Saturn. This may seem 'bad,' but you cannot have greatness and good things without negative ones. Saturn ensures this balance and will manifest in your life in serious ways to balance your energy, often through tough tasks or boundaries. The organizational quality of Saturn will teach lessons and show you that nothing lasts forever. Be sure to be serious and disciplined when working with Saturn.

Day: Saturday
Number: 8
Exalted: Libra

Mars
The red planet Mars is often thought to be the opposing force to Venus's beauty and grace. Mars is violent and malefic, with a tendency to be aggressive and conflicted. The physical energy of Mars manifests on earth as war or other violent actions. The sex drive is governed by Mars, as well as the ability to be assertive enough to initiate social interactions, whether romantic or platonic. Passionate drive and motivation are dictated by your Mars placement. How you use your free will to initiate action is representative of Mars's placement in your natal chart. At its worse, Mars can influence someone to be overly aggressive or easily angered for unjustified reasons. This force is one to be very aware of, if you have an unfavorable Mars transit taking place then you may have just a day or two of aggression and combative behavior, by studying your chart and keeping an eye on Mars you may be able to prepare for these transits and better balance them out to avoid any manifestations of trouble. Mars completes its journey through the signs in two years.

Two years
Day: Tuesday
Number: 9
Exalted: Capricorn

Pluto

The planet Pluto has been declassified as a planet recently, but this doesn't mean his influence is any less important. In fact, many celestial bodies within our solar system are considered influential, but asteroids and other bodies are reserved for more advanced astrology. Pluto itself represents an unconscious desire to make a lasting impression on society. This transformative effect empowers one to accomplish as much as possible. Pluto is the slowest moving planet from our perspective on earth; this 248-year journey means that Pluto stays in the same sign for a very long time. Therefore, entire generations of people have identical Pluto placement in their natal charts; this makes Pluto a great representative of social uproar and the transformative effects that younger generations impart onto society. Pluto has such a broad effect on our lives that it can alter the course of history with its transformational energy.

On a personal level, Pluto's energy is manifested through personal growth and regeneration. Emotional crisis and unexpected drama are minions of Pluto's effects, but more often than not after enduring these troublesome times new insight and knowledge are gained. This is transformative and healing, even if the positive effects are not immediately noticeable. An unbalanced Pluto placement or overly Plutonian influence may lead to reckless behavior or emotional obsessions.

Day
Number
Stones
Exalted
Detriment

Rahu & Ketu

Before the discovery of planets that are too far away from earth to be seen with the naked eye, the north and south nodes of the moon were assigned the numerology that now gets assigned to Uranus and Neptune. These nodes are points where the paths of the sun and moon intersect. The use of these nodes is popular in the Vedic system, but they are not found in some older texts. These nodes offer insight into these influences that are so closely associated with the powerful sun and moon. Eclipses are typically associated with these energies as well.

These two nodes are often considered to parts of one whole, symbolized by a dragon. Although some systems disagree, these nodes do not aspect other planets and do not rule zodiac signs. Let's touch on the influence that Rahu and Ketu have and how they interact with the other planets.

Rahu
The north node of the moon is associated with Rahu or the dragon's head. When the moon is moving south to north, the point where it crosses the sun's path is Rahu. If the sun or moon are conjunct with Rahu, a solar eclipse occurs. Rahu is intellectually reasonable and focuses much influence on material matters.

Ketu
The south node of the moon is called Ketu or the dragon's tail. When the moon is moving north to South and crosses the path of the sun, this is Ketu. The influence of Ketu is determined to bring lessons from past lives into consciousness. Eliminating emotional weight and guilty memories are supported by Ketu. As opposed to Rahu's earthly regards, Ketu is very much concerned with spiritual matters.

Houses

In astrology, houses are twelve subdivisions that planets and signs move within. These houses usually represent different broad areas of life, for instance, the 2nd house deals with money and self-worth. So a planet will be in a sign of the zodiac that will, in turn, be within a house. The nature of the zodiac sign and the planet will predominantly affect the area of life that the house represents.

These houses are also ruled by certain planets; this means the planet is 'home' and thus more concentrated influence of the planet is present. This also means there is a detrimental placement where the planet is weakest. Let's take a look at the twelve houses and what areas of life they govern.

First House
The First house governs appearances, both physical and mental. How you view yourself and what you present to others. First impressions, pet peeves, our investment in our surroundings, and overall personality. The way you carry yourself and how others see you are the general areas of life this house governs. This manifests as someone's 'energy' or how they feel as they enter the room. Your literal appearance is affected as well. Early upbringing and environment in early life are manifestations of this house as well.

Ruler: Aries
Keywords: Self, appearances, image, environment, head, ego, and mannerisms

Second House
The second house governs wealth. Financial wealth, emotional wealth and anything that is valued are affected by this house placement. These influences manifest by our ability to save money, our spending habits and investments. Our compassion is tested in this house as we send life accumulating loved ones or pushing them away. Our collections and possessions are manifestations of this house placement as well. Faith and worldview are affected as spiritual wealth.

Ruler: Taurus
Keywords: Money, worth, value, possessions, security

Third House
The third house governs communications, interactions with others and interactions with our environment. Inner dialogue is affected as well as how you use words in any way. This includes speech, text messages and writing. Casual conversation and small talk are manifestations of this house's placement. How well you can express your emotions and examine other people's communications are other areas dictated by this house and the planets within it.

Ruler: Gemini
Keywords: Communication, brothers and sisters, speaking, short travel

Fourth House
The fourth house governs the roots of your existence, your ancestry, home life, family and culture. Instincts and fight or flight is affected by this house and the planets within it. These deep-rooted areas of life are often masked by the influence of society and may need to be 'dug up' or explored. Home life and private life are governed by this house as well. Parenthood and the ability to nurture and provide security are other life areas supported by the fourth house

Ruler: Cancer
Keywords: Foundation, security, Parenting, roots, privacy

Fifth House
The fifth house governs your ability to express yourself. Whether it's an artistic expression of simply trying to explain how you feel, this house affects any type of expression. Expressing love and romance is supported by this house, as well as the ability to play and let loose. Attentiveness and dramatic events are also greatly affected by the fifth house.

Ruler: Leo
Keywords: Expression, romance, play, drama

Sixth House
The sixth house governs contribution to society and healthfulness. Charitable contributions and other services are supported by this house. Organizational skills, any routine, exercise and general health are greatly affected by this house and the planets therein. The ability to be selfless and help others is the territory of the sixth house; this humility comes with a balanced combination of planets or transits in this house.

Ruler: Virgo
Keywords: Health, routine, humility, service

Seventh House
The seventh house rules relationships and your connection to other people. Any pairing, whether it's platonic, romantic or business is

affected by this house and the planets placed within. Contracts, agreements, marriages and promises are supported by this house. Essentially any meeting or any agreement you make, even small ones, are supported by this house.

Ruler: Libra
Keywords: Relations, connection, agreements, contracts, promises

Eighth House
The eight house is a unique house, governing death, sex and birth. These transformative acts are a crucial part of life that are often ignored or considered negative. Any mysterious area of life is affected by the eight house. Intimacy with depth and meaning I supported by this house. This house also rules monetary gain, material possessions and other belongings.

Ruler: Scorpio
Keywords: Sex, death, birth, money, mystery

Ninth House
This ninth house governs spiritual and mindful progress. These higher states of thinking and thriving in other realms add an open-minded perspective. This leads the house to also affect prejudice, long journeys, and the exploration of cultures, philosophical aspirations and religious choices. Justice and morality are also supported by this house.

Ruler: Sagittarius
Keywords: Morality, higher thinking, adventure, education

Tenth House
The tenth house governs public appearance, large companies, governments and overall how you are presented on a world scale. Fame and fortune, popularity and public achievements are aspects of this house as well. Restrictions, boundaries and authority are also supported by this house. Career choices may also be affected by this house. A unique aspect of this house is that the cusp of the tenth house is named the Midheaven, the position of this point in your chart will greatly affect a favorable career choice.

Ruler: Capricorn

Keywords: Boundary, World events, popularity, career

Eleventh House
The eleventh house governs teamwork, friendship, group work and overall acceptance into various groups. Societal standards, social politics and rebellious movements are also supported by this house. Original creative endeavors and eccentric behavior also are areas of life that are affected by this house. Surprises, unexpected events and inventive ideas find their home is this sector as well. Futurism and technological progression also live in the eleventh house.

Ruler: Aquarius
Keywords: Future, science, teamwork, humanitarianism

Twelfth House
The twelfth house is the final house; it governs the completion of things. Finished tasks, ending relationships and the afterlife all are housed here. Growing old, surrendering to time and endings, in general, are supported by this house. Introverted behavior, loneliness and separation from the world are all affected by this house. Artistic endeavors such as dance, painting and creative writing are all ruled by this house and the planets therein.

Ruler: Pisces
Keywords: Art, separation, old age, completion

Vocabulary

Below are some keywords that may be specific to astrology or need some defining. This list is made to be an easy reference for astrological vocabulary.

Stellium

This word refers to the occurrence when three or more planets occupy a certain sign. There is much debate on how many planets define a stellium; some astrologers say it's two to three and others believe there needs to be four or more planets in one sign to be considered a stellium.

Ascendant

The ascendant is also known as the 'rising sign.' This is the ascending sign that the horizon crosses through as your looking at the night sky. The influence of the ascendant is likened to a mask worn while socializing or working. This mask is a defense mechanism used to cope with everyday stress; it is your immediate reaction to your surroundings.

Aspect

Aspects are certain powerful angles that planets can be from each other. When planets are positioned a certain number of degrees from each other, they create an aspect. The most prominent aspects are conjunct, sextile, trine, square, opposing.

Configuration

An aspect between three planets or more.

Cusp

The dividing line between the twelve signs. If a planet is within a degree or two of the cusp, it is considered 'on the cusp' and may have the influence of being in both signs. Many astrologers debate whether or not this actually makes any difference. They also debate on how many degrees a planet would have to be within to be considered on the cusp.

Cycle

The amount of time it takes a planet to complete its journey through the zodiac.

Decan

Decans are found in Egyptian astrology; they further divide up the signs into three 10-degree sections. Each section has a more specific influence than simply the sign's broad influence.

Degrees

The zodiac consists of 360 degrees. As planets pass through the zodiac, they move through each degree. Degrees allow us to pinpoint the exact placement of planets in a sign.

Descendant

The opposite sign that the horizon passes through at the time of your birth is the descendant. This is considered to be a shadow self; these are the behaviors and personalities we are not. These may be repressed behaviors, good and bad, or even memories that we refuse to acknowledge. The descendant is always the opposite sign of the ascendant.

Ephemeris

An astrological almanac that documents a year's astrological weather.

Equinox

A day where there are equal parts day and night. There are two equinoxes per year, one in spring and one in autumn.

Fixed signs

Fixed signs of the zodiac are stubborn. Taurus, Leo, Scorpio

Grand Trine
When three Planets are trine to each other in the same elemental sign.

Lilith
Also known as the black moon, this is thought to be either an invisible energy vortex or an asteroid named Lilith. Not all systems adhere to this idea.

Lunar Mansions

The zodiac divided into 27 sections; this follows where the moon spends most of her time on a daily basis. Some systems use a 28-day version; this is similar to following a moon calendar.

Mutable Signs
Mutable signs are flexible and open to change, Gemini, Virgo, Sagittarius and Pisces

Native
You are a native to the planetary ruler of the sign that your ascendant is in. This means that this sign is going to affect your outward self and be more obvious to others, even more so than the sun sign at times. For example, if your ascendant sign is Capricorn, then you are a Saturn native.

Opposition Aspect
An aspect called opposition is created when two planets are 180 degrees apart. This creates opposing forces and be combative in nature.

Progressions
Using progressions is a form of forecasting astrology. This is done by progressing your chart forward, either on day per year, or one degree per year. The resulting chart can be used to predict events and major occurrences.

Qualities
Qualities of a sign can be mutable, fixed, or cardinal

Retrograde
When a planet appears to be moving in the opposite direction than normal. This concentrates the energy as if the planet is 'swiping' back and forth in one or two signs.

Rulership
Signs have planetary rulers that they are exalted in.

Solstice

There are two solstices per year, one in summer and one in winter. The Summer solstice occurs when there is the longest amount of daylight. The Winter solstice occurs when there is the least amount of daylight.

Transit
When planet moves through a sign or house, it is called a transit. There are also natal transits where a planet moves past the position of one of your natal planets.

Void of Course
Mainly referring to the moon, this term describes a planet that does not have a major aspect before changing signs.

The Elements

The idea of elements is an ancient one; many cultures believe that a handful of elements make-up the true nature of reality. These elements are Earth, Air, Fire and Water respectively. Ether, wood or metal may also be found as elements in some systems. Each sign of the zodiac is attributed to a specific element; this is symbolic of its general behavior. Each of these signs will also have a certain quality either cardinal, fixed or mutable.

Earth Signs
Taurus (fixed) – Virgo (Mutable) – Capricorn (Cardinal)

This element governs practicality and reason.

Air Signs
Gemini (Mutable) – Libra (Cardinal) – Aquarius (fixed)
The element of air governs intellect and thought processes.

Fire
Aries (Cardinal) – Leo (Fixed) – Sagittarius (Mutable)
This element governs passion and temperament.

Water
Cancer (Cardinal) – Scorpio (Fixed) – Pisces (Mutable)
This element governs intuition and emotions.

CHAPTER 5
The Zodiac

You've probably used horoscopes before, perhaps in the back of a popular magazine or online. These simple astrological reviews are based on the twelve signs of the zodiac. Horoscopes draw vague, and often fun, conclusions about a person's life based on what sign in the zodiac the sun was positioned in when they were born. These practices are relatively simple, but the zodiac is much more complex than general assumptions about one's love life.

From our perspective here on earth, the zodiac is a path that the sun travels across the sky. As he travels, he passes through twelve different sections of the sky each one with a constellation of stars that also appear to move across the sky in the opposite direction. The constellations are as follows starting with the sun's 'home' in Aries then; Taurus, Gemini, Cancer, Leo, Virgo, Libra, Scorpio, Sagittarius, Capricorn, Aquarius, and Pisces. After this, we return to Aries. All planets in our solar system are moving within the sphere of these constellations respectively.

Although from our perspective it may seem like the heavens are moving around the earth, but we know now that the earth itself is moving around the sun. These patterns create a dance in the sky, and when studied can lead to correlated patterns to events on earth. And although many popular horoscopes are based around where the sun is positioned, all the other planets have influence over other parts of our lives creating a quite complicated equation.

The zodiac has become a household term in the western world ever since the influx of horoscope astrology and other celestial practices became popular in the 1970s. Although the ideas and use of the zodiac are centuries old, it has only been used in popular culture since its rise in popularity in the past few decades. Let's explore its history and use.

The Signs
Each of the twelve signs of the zodiac has their own distinct set of traits. Each one comes equipped with a sigil, an animal image,

color, number, planetary ruler, element, part of the human body, and many other personality traits that make the sign unique. With the study of these signs, we not only learn about the nature of reality itself but also of our true nature depending on the sign's influence over our lives.

Most popular horoscopes are written using the Sun sign only. Although where the sun is placed in the chart is very important, it is not the only planetary influence that needs to be considered. Horoscopes can be fun and give a broad insight into sun influence if written well, but to get the most out of astrology, we need to learn about all the signs and the planets placed within them in our natal chart. This being said, we need to keep in mind that no person is purely an Aries or Taurus; all the signs play a role in influencing your life. Even if there is no planet in a certain sign in your natal chart, there will typically be a transit or aspect in those signs at some point in your life.

Below we will list the signs and give a broad overview of what area of life the sign governs. Each sign has its own unique influence over certain behaviors, this plus the influence and support form houses and of course planets creates a complex combination of influences. Study these signs and make it a point to follow the sun or moon through these signs on a daily basis, this will help you get to know them and learn their personalities so you may better work with them throughout your life.

Aries
Ram – Cardinal Fire – Ruler: Mars

Aries is considered the first astrological month and begins right after the spring equinox. This lengthening of daylight is fitting for fiery Aries, the sun is making its way to exaltation and will exalt in another fire sign, Leo. The goat is used as the animal image for Aries since the Aries influence is energetic and always needing to move. Courageous and full of life, Aries is competitive and absolutely loves to win. Leadership roles and creative ways of solving problems are other Aries influences. As with other fire signs, Aries is impatient but warm, impulsive and excitable, and yet the optimistic approach to life is very welcoming at times. Spontaneous fits of temper are common for Aries but never lasts too long, Aries is very forgivable and never remains sad or angry for long periods of time.

Taurus
Bull – Fixed Earth – Ruler: Venus

The Taurus influence is patient and peaceful, but when excited can be very assertive. Relaxed at most times, the Taurus influence enjoys sensual pleasures especially food and viewing beautiful artwork or music. Stability and comfort are a must for Taurus to be happy and he's more than content to put in some hard work to achieve his creature comforts. If excited this sign is best avoided, not unlike an actual bull, you do not want to be on the receiving end of his temper. Rural areas are favored by Taurus; cities tend to be anxious and fast-paced, not his favorite atmosphere. While this influence offers talents in art and craftsmanship, some may find it difficult to decide on a career path; the calm bull is in no hurry to make decisions. Reliability and a firm foundation come along with this earth sign's demeanor.

Gemini
Twins – Mutable air – Ruler: Mercury

Gemini has a tendency to offer talents in writing and teaching. The image of the twins is very fitting since Gemini loves to share with others. Communication is a key influence from the twins and this is often manifested as a caring and open personality. Curiosity and a general interest in everything, Gemini loves to chat with friends or acquaintances about any topic. Being alone is not favored by the Gemini influence; this makes for a healthy social life and large friend circles. Knowledge on a variety of topics makes Gemini influenced people very fun to be around; they are very engaging and can find a way to connect very easily. Typically, up to date on current trends and culture, Gemini enjoys discussing art, politics and world events. Traveling and exploring new cultures is a must for the Gemini.

Cancer
Crab – Cardinal Water – Ruler: Moon

The influence of Cancer is mirrored by the behavior of crabs. Its home is wherever he is and if need be, he can cling very tightly to something he wants. This is common behavior for Cancer influenced people, often moving from home to home and being stubborn if he can't get his way. Cancers are family-oriented but tend to be passive in communication, often going out of their way to avoid confrontation. Family and relationships are coveted by cancer and he desperately tries to not lose any friends or family by trying to please them even if he may disagree or not want to directly confront the situation. The behavior of Cancer can be very needy, requiring lots of attention and confirmation from loved ones. They need security to compensate for their passive and sensitive approach to life. Although often reserved, when relaxed Cancer can be very fun loving and talented, with a deep insight that comes along with the support of the water element.

Leo
Lion – Fixed Fire – Ruler: Sun

The influence of Leo is proud and energetic; this sign offers a sense of dignity and confidence. The Lion is an obvious match for this sign; the king of the jungle knows what he wants and knows how to get it. All aspects of Leo are confident, communication, demeanor and even appearances can invoke confidence. Although serious and balanced the lion enjoys relaxation and playfulness as well. This makes for a combination that is perfect for careers that require leadership or performance. Leo loves attention and often can be cranky if their desire for it isn't fulfilled. Little tasks and mundane events are of no concern for Leos; they predominantly of the big picture and do not like being bossed around. Leo is always seeking love and attention, always checking to see if they are being watched, and hoping for approval from an outside perspective. Leo may present an overly self-involved influence; it is important for people with heavy Leo placement to realize that while they love the attention, other people need some love also.

Virgo
Maiden – Mutable Earth – Ruler: Mercury

The influence of Virgo is clear-headedness and the ability to be as one pointed as necessary. Virgo is gentle and soft-spoken, with a quiet demeanor that may seem like shyness, but typically isn't the case. The thoughtful maiden is usually contemplating or listening rather than avoiding the situation. They love crafts and are willing to work hard to create beauty through artistic endeavor. This quiet and craft attitude is perfect for being alone, and Virgo spends her time alone wisely. While being alone is fine for the maiden, she also wishes to contribute to society in meaningful ways. Service jobs and charitable causes are ideal for Virgo to ensure that their time alone isn't consuming their life. This balance is the lesson of Virgo. The Earth element contributes to this selfless mindset. Earth signs love to help others as much as possible.

Libra

Scales – Cardinal Air – Ruler: Venus

The influence of Libra is symbolized by a set of scales for a reason, Libra values balance and aims to create balance every moment throughout life. Work versus play is a big struggle for many people and Libra knows how to balance these two perfectly. Libra can also see the balance of positivity and negativity in everyday life, knowing that happiness is not possible without sadness. This balanced mindset may make it tough for Libra to make decisions; this is a result of being able to quickly weigh the positive and negative sides of any given situation. The focus on harmony is great for the Libra in relationships, striving for balance; they know how to handle emotional situations and find the balance within them. Libra will not tolerate a one-sided relationship and cannot put up with not being appreciated. Libras love art and prefer harmonious music as compared to dissonance or disruptive themes. Science and mathematics are appealing to Libra since there is a solidly constructed rulebook for these practices. The Air element adds to the love of harmony as well, the 'floating on air' feeling when everything is perfectly balanced.

Scorpio

Scorpion – Fixed Water – Ruler: Pluto

The influence of Scorpio offers behavior that is contemplative and serious. He needs time to think deeply about things before he acts; this allows him to be meticulous and focused. Not unlike an actual scorpion, Scorpio can be dangerous if angered or betrayed. Don't be fooled by Scorpio's shy and quiet demeanor; he is intense and very good at deception or learning secrets. He can see through other people's deception very easily and knows how to understand their deceit. Scorpio is not easily frightened; they defend themselves and their loved ones with assertion and fortitude. Scorpio seeks justice in all areas of life; his deep thought offers much time to analyze society and the injustices within. The intense depth of thought also leads Scorpio to influence our lives in a way that requires us to understand our true selves. People with a heavy Scorpio influence spend a lot of time analyzing their past actions and the present effects of the actions. Careers that require seriousness and deep studies are suitable for Scorpio, surgeons, psychiatry and other healing careers are perfect. As a water sign Scorpio offers a heightened sensitivity as well, so tread lightly not to anger him.

Sagittarius

Centaur – Mutable Fire – Ruler: Jupiter

The influence of Sagittarius is adventurous and social. This optimistic sign is symbolized by the Centaur, a mythological creature that is half man and half horse. This creature roams the earth on adventures simply seeking joy and new experience. The Centaur carries a bow and arrow; this is symbolic of choosing goals and attaining them. Imagine the centaur firing his arrow, only to chase it down and shoot again. This pursuit of adventurous goals is personified in people who have a heavy Sagittarian influence. This adventurous spirit requires a nomadic attitude and plenty of freedom. If Sagittarius is not free to do as he pleases, then he is left unfulfilled and distressed. The desire to keep moving is not only physical but mental as well. Some may find themselves unable to finish projects before starting new ones, leaving many goals unattended too. This is the lesson of Sagittarius, to complete what you started. World culture and athletics are of much interest to Sagittarius; they love playing and having fun in general. Sagittarius is an obvious Fire sign, travel and constant movement are required for fulfillment, while confidence guides the way.

Capricorn
Goat-mermaid – Cardinal Earth – Ruler: Saturn

The influence of Capricorn is filled with structure and logic. This Saturn ruled sign is serious and goal oriented. The mountain goat is the symbolic image for Capricorn, not only a goat but also a mermaid; this is curious as a mythological creature associated with death and the underworld. Capricorn is self-disciplined and supports boundaries and restrictions in the form of goals and desired achievement. The Capricorn influence offers skills in craftsmanship and overall any line of work that requires hard work. A career in law or politics is favorable for Capricorn. Diplomacy and reason are attributed to this sign as well. The use of well thought out tactics and defense are common among those with heavy Capricorn influence; they tend to be tough to read and rarely let their guards down. With the Earth influence Capricorn is equipped with a level head and great family skills, often the voice of reason during dramatic family events.

Aquarius
Water bearer – Fixed Air – Ruler: Uranus

The influence of Aquarius is genuinely concerned for the well-being of others. Aquarius readily offers gifts to those in need and happily would give their last drop of water to someone rather than drink it themselves. This selflessness and lack of prejudice is the lesson of Aquarius, trying not to exhaust themselves by attempting to help everyone all the time. The friendly and clever Aquarius may be excellent inventors and love new technological gadgetry. They may even be involved in politics, offering their sense of justice and genuine love of people as a means of diplomacy. Aquarius is empathetic as well, offering a heightened ability to sense the feelings of others. Aquarius does not judge others by their appearances and gives the benefit of the doubt in most situations. This water bearer is happy to nourish the world with much-needed waters, often in the form of a charitable cause or a simple, friendly smile.

Pisces
Fish – Mutable Water – Ruler: Neptune

The influence of Pisces is graceful and secretive. The mysteries of the ocean and its beautiful rhythm makes the fish a suitable image for the Pisces attitude. Pisces loves the arts, especially art with esoteric themes and abstract ideas that can be interpreted any number of ways. Their private internal reality is rarely shared with others; they hold their secrets dear and are not concerned with impressing others with their valuable perspective. Pisces enjoys helping the downtrodden, often going out of their way to cheer someone up with a joke or fun gesture. Pisces is often misunderstood due to the secrecy of their inner dialogue; this can lead to trouble making connections with others. Their knowledge of the mysteries of life and natural magic are often seen as ridiculous and can push away some of the more skeptical types of people. Pisces is very loving and sometimes can find a way to securely share their inner dialogue through writing or artistic endeavors. Imaginative and open to the mysterious nature of the world, Pisces holds important gifts that are attainable you are trustworthy and humble.

CHAPTER 6
Your Astrology

As we have seen, there is a lot to consider when it comes to learning your personal astrology. There is a lifetime's worth of studying that could be done to analyze the heavens and how they affect you and your surroundings. Many people memorize their sun sign and leave it at that; this is only scratching the surface of your specific astrology. While memorizing all the planets at once is a daunting task, it is recommended that starting with the sun, moon, and ascendant be studied first since they have some of the most influential qualities of the natal chart.

Learning this esoteric art is a lifelong task, but there are many simple ways to implement astrology into your life. Timing certain events, predicting the future and working with the specific planets and signs to improve yourself are only a few practices in the expanse of the heavens. While there is no reason for us to go into why or how it works, there are many theories. Some believe that the planets and stars have an actual physical effect on the earth and its inhabitants. Some believe that some actual gods or spirits reside on or in these planets in dimensions humans cannot see. Others believe that the heavens simply offer insight into ourselves and acts as a symbolic mirror of events on earth. Perhaps it is simply a very efficient calendar. Maybe it is all these things. Regardless of what you choose to believe about the true nature of reality, astrology will help you in some way. Whether it's communicating with spirits or just psychological analysis, the heavens are powerful and if you pay attention to them, they will pay attention to you.

In today's society, we can simply use technology to help us keep track of our personal chart and any transits. It is highly recommended that you download an astrology app that calculates your natal chart and offers some insight into its aspects. There are many, many apps so try a few and pick one that suits you. These apps often have notifications that will keep track of any powerful transits or world events, such as a full moon or disruptive Uranus transiting your natal Mars.

Below we will discuss certain techniques and practices that are common when working with the planets and stars. These techniques are as old as time itself, but we will filter them through a contemporary lens. Use these techniques wisely and be humble when approaching these energies, there are plenty of shared experiences, old and new, that may be adverse effects of using astrology for evil purposes. Be morally upstanding and appreciative of the gifts that the heavens offer.

Your signs

As we mentioned, your sun sign, moon sign and ascendant are the best starting points to begin your journey into astrology. Let's take a look at these influences with more in-depth detail.

Sun Sign

You may know your sun sign already. The sun sign is the sign the sun was placed in at the exact time of your birth. This is what most astrology sites use to write up horoscopes and other personality traits. While the sun sign is probably one of the most important signs, we need to consider all the other planets as well, but this requires a computer program or intense math to calculate. Since our current society relies on a sun-based calendar, we can know what our sun sign is using our well-known twelve-month calendar. The sun signs are as follows:

Aries: March 21 – April 19
Taurus: April 20 – May 20
Gemini: May 21 – June 20
Cancer: June 21 – July 22
Leo: July 23 - August 22)
Virgo: August 23 - September 22
Libra: September 23 - October 22
Scorpio: October 23 - November 21
Sagittarius: November 22 - December 21
Capricorn: December 22 - January 19
Aquarius: January 20 - February 18
Pisces: February 19 - March 20

Find your birthdate and keep a note of your sun sign. Go back to the zodiac and planets section of this book and read up on the qualities of this sign and the sun. Do you see parallels in your life? Are these readings somewhat accurate? Don't be discouraged if it's not describing you in detail; there are many other astrological factors as well that influence your natural makeup.

Take note of the positive and negative effects of certain planets; sometimes you may find yourself being grumpy or unnecessarily upset. Before you are quick to blame yourself, check your natal chart. Perhaps there's an emotional transit in Cancer or a fiery Mars transit. This is one technique that helps balance your emotional state, instead of getting down on yourself you will see that there are some rough waters ahead in your chart, you will be able to prepare for these times, maybe plan some relaxation time, or give offerings to the troubling planet as a means to soften the blow.

Moon Sign

The moon sign is more complicated to calculate since our calendar doesn't sync up with its cycles as well. We can check our moon sign online or with an app. Once you find your moon sign, check the zodiac and planets section to cross reference the personality traits. The moon moves quite quickly through the zodiac so the more will transit your natal moon about once per solar month. This conjunct aspect will create harmonious moon energy for a couple of days. The phase of the moon will affect this as well, this is easily known by looking up at the night sky, but can also be found out with an app or internet search.

The moon is so fluid that her personality and influence is constantly changing. It is no secret that a full moon night is always a strange one. Depending on what sign the full moon is in, these nights are great for moon workings. Festive socializing and indulgence are common on full moon nights, so if you are trying to plan a party and want to choose a favorable date, choose the next full moon, see what sign it will be in and plan accordingly. Leave an offering for the moon that evening and ask for her good grace.

Aspects

An astrological aspect is a number of degrees that a planet may be from another planet; this creates an angle that has a certain effect on the planet's relationship to each other. These angles can be between two planets or even a planet and the ascendant. These aspects are either considered hard aspects or soft aspects, the hard aspects being more intensive respectfully.

These aspects happen throughout the planetary movement, although some days may not have any notable aspects at all, this is considered relatively calm skies. Planets can be aspect to each other in real time or even create an aspect to your natal planets; for example, Venus could create an aspect to your natal Venus. Aspects also have a specific house they are linked to. Your natal chart will also more than likely have aspects between planets, so it is good to familiarize yourself with how these aspects alter the planet's personalities. Let's explore the hard aspects and their influences.

Conjunction

When planets are conjunct, they are very close to each other in the chart, usually within ten degrees of each other. This aspect is thought to be one of the most powerful aspects any two planets can create. Conjunct planets typically have a harmonious quality as the planets work together to create a distinct influence. Depending on the sign that they are conjunct in the planets could work together to because you trouble as well, this is also dependent on your natal chart as well. It needs to be said that sometimes more than two planets can be conjunct to each other. Three or even four planets could be within a few degrees of each other; this can be very complex and intense energy. If three or more planets are conjunct in a natal chart, it is called a stellium. Conjunct aspects are closely linked to the 1st house

Sextile

When planets are sixty degrees apart, it is called a sextile aspect. This aspect is considered to be creative and dynamic, often dealing with groups or teamwork. Ease of communication between the planets involved and overall favorable unless poorly represented in your natal chart. This aspect is closely linked to the 3rd and 11th houses.

Square

When planets are ninety degrees apart, they are considered a square aspect. It is thought that if an outer planet, Jupiter, Saturn, Uranus, Neptune or Pluto is square an inner planet then the outer planet is usually affecting the inner planet more intensely. This aspect often lends itself to troubling or complicated decision making. This could cause conflict or dramatic crisis. This aspect is closely linked to the 4th and 10th houses.

Trine

When planets are one-hundred-twenty degrees from each other, they are considered to be trine. We see the power of three come into play with this aspect; it is considered to be harmonious and progressive, often awakening inner desires or talents that have been dormant. Peace of mind and calming of the storms is brought with this aspect. Conflicts are resolved and expression comes easily. This aspect is closely linked to the 5th and 9th houses.

Opposition

When planets are one hundred and eighty degrees from each other, or directly across from each other in a chart, they are considered to be in opposition. Unlike the unification effects of conjunction, opposition aspects create polarity and tension. This can be conflicting, creating a battle between internal and external forces. This isn't necessarily always negative, sometimes opposites attract for a distinct reason, commonly to teach a lesson through intense experience or trying times. This aspect is closely related to the 7th house.

Minor aspects

We have explored the major aspects, but there are minor aspects as well. Many astrologers agree that these aspects are miniscule and have a very subtle effect that may not be worth too much time and attention. Some minor aspects are as follows:

Semi-Sextile – Thirty-degree angle
Quintile – Seventy-two-degree angle
Septile – fifty- one-degree angle
Semi-square – Forty-five-degree angle

We see with these aspects that astrology can get very complex, one may say almost as complex as human personalities. This realization solidifies the fact that sun sign horoscopes and readings alone are not in depth enough to really get any insight into someone's complicated personality. This is why we suggest focusing on the three major astrological planets, sun, moon and ascendant when you are beginning in astrology.

Planetary Hours

Similar to how each day has a planetary ruler, Sunday/Sun, each hour of the day is ruled by a certain planet as well. The order of planets is the same each day but will start with a different planet depending on what day it is. This further details a planet's influence throughout the day, so if a planet is ruling a certain hour, then that planet is that much more influential during that hour. This system uses only the seven classical planets, so Uranus, Neptune and Pluto are left out. The order of planets is known as the Chaldean Order; this comes from ancient Babylonian astrology. The order was developed by taking how long each planet takes to travel the entire zodiac, the slowest to quickest planets as they appear from the earth's perspective. We see an order of planets with our naming of the weekdays Sunday through Saturday, but for planetary hours we will skip three planets backward in this list to know the next hour's ruler. For example, Tuesday is ruled by Mars, so around daybreak, the hour of Mars begins. The next hour will be the hour of the sun since we skip three planets previous of the weekday order:

Sunday – Sun 3
Monday – Moon 2
Tuesday – Mars 1
Wednesday - Mercury

Thursday - Jupiter
Friday – Venus
Saturday – Saturn

And so the order of planetary hours for Tuesday will go:

Mars
Sun
Venus
Mercury
Moon
Saturn
Jupiter

This pattern is the same every day only starting with the ruler of that day. This syncs up with our current order of the weekdays so that every twenty-fifth hour is the following day's planetary ruler and thus a new cycle.
The planetary hours are great for timing certain things. If you are looking to work with the moon, choosing a Monday in the hour of the moon to leave offerings or initiate an activity that is governed by the moon, such as taking a bath, is the most potent. This is why we see a lot of planetary rituals and prayers performed at daybreak or dusk; this hour of the day is usually ruled by that day's planetary ruler.

Practice

So how can you apply what you've learned to better yourself and your life? There are many ways to go about this, ancient and more contemporary. Also, keep in mind that you create your own practice as well, there is nothing wrong with an individual routine or technique that you created. If it works, then it works. Let's explore some common uses for astrology in the real world for self-development and personal empowerment.

Timing
Sometimes it can be tough to decide when to start a new project, or plan that dinner date. Many people probably do not pay any mind to the fact that if you plan something on an astrologically

unfavorable day that it may not go well. Using your natal chart and current chart will help with this.

For example, if you were wanting to get married, it is recommended to so on a favorable day. Don't pick a day when Mars is excited and going to cause conflict and troubles. If you can plan it on a day when Venus is in the 7th house, on the day of Venus, in the hour of Venus then you have a powerful combination for love and marriage, also leaving offerings for Venus will help gain good grace from the beauteous planet.

Take time to plan all major events in this way; it may take more time to plan but imagine how much time you lose when things don't go according to your expectations! Be sure to look at the current configurations of planets. Many apps allow you to cycle ahead and see what the configurations will be on any given day. Pick a time when a favorable planet is in the most suitable house and doesn't have any negative aspects. It also encouraged to keep retrogrades in mind, for instance starting new projects or long journeys is not recommended during Mercury in retrograde.

Offerings

Although some people that practice astrology don't adhere to this practice, many ancient systems felt that there were gods or spirits that act as mediators between humans and the heavens. Our ancestors would leave offerings and say prayers for the planets to appease them and avid troubling aspects. This practice is great for the spiritual side of astrology and at the very least helps you build a relationship with the planets.

Setting up a planetary altar to leave offerings at is very useful, although you may leave the offerings outdoors as well. For example, let's use the planet Jupiter. On Jupiter's day, in the hour of Jupiter, light a candle that is white or a color associated with Jupiter, such as a royal purple. While the candle is lit, you can meditate in Jupiter and his personality, maybe say a prayer or ask his good grace. Suitable offerings for any planet include incense, coins, water or herbs. For Jupiter money is ideal, especially if you are seeking material gains from this Jupiter working. Finish up your quiet moment with Jupiter and give thanks. Leave the candlelit if you'd like, or blow it out for future use.

With this practice, it is highly suggested that you study astrological magick to make sure you want to take this route. This type of work is very transformative and should be handled with great care and humility. Be respectful and keep in mind this is not a game; once you start this journey you have the planet's attention, do not ignore them.

World Events

To fill time in between your personal work many astrologers analyze world events. You can pick a major event and calculate its astrology and see how it syncs up with the planetary configuration. This helps you understand the planets and zodiac from a broader perspective. Many choose to calculate the president's natal charts or major shifts in civilization. This can be done for past events or to forecast future events, which we will explore deeper in subsequent chapters.

CHAPTER 7
Tarot

The mysterious and powerful tarot cards are infamous for being used to predict the future or even gain insight into one's personal life. This deck of cards has been used by humans for centuries. Of the Divinatory arts tarot finds its place among runes, crystal balls, tea leaf reading and palm reading. But the tarot is much more curious and seems to have a mind of its own as it travels through the centuries.

Even traditional playing cards for poker and other popular games find their roots in the tarot, but this art is no child's game. The power of numbers, images and the powerful faculties of the human mind combine to develop a practice that is cherished by occultists and popular culture alike. The tarot may be found in movies and television alongside monsters and ghosts, but its history is very real and so is its powers to give insight into the human condition, as well as the true nature of reality.

There are thousands of tarot decks, from medieval Italian decks to contemporary decks that have images of cats or your favorite flowers. Many people that study the tarot question the powerful potential of themed decks that have dogs or dragons. Can these decks hold the same power as centuries-old decks? Or are these just fun decks for collectors and artists? These are questions that you can answer on your own, remember, if it works, it works.

What is the Tarot?

There are many different tarot decks in the world. Some are made for games and some for specific collectors of cards. For our intents and purposes, we will be focusing on esoteric tarot and its use for divination, or the practice of gaining knowledge of the future through communion with spirits or other supernatural forces.

Some practitioners of tarot hold the esoteric belief that the cards hold all human knowledge and lessons. It is said that if a person were to be sheltered from the world and any teachings in religion or philosophy and they were to be given a tarot deck that they could learn the secrets of the world just by meditating on the images and numerological attributions. This is legendary in its powers, but these secrets are not easily known. It takes years of practice and commitment to reveal these mysteries. The tarot can speak to you through its contemplation, but to truly know the truths of the universe will take a perspective and open heart that is not simply attained at birth.

Many use the tarot to answer tough questions or to gain insight into future events. How this art works is unknown, some believe the cards act as a catalyst into the spirit realms. Others feel that the cards unlock secrets inside the human mind in the form of Jungian archetypes, perhaps it's both.

The tarot can contain any number of cards, but traditionally for divination and forecasting, a seventy-eight-card deck is used. These seventy-eight cards are divided into two sections, the major arcana and the minor arcana. These two groups have their own respective intentions and powers. Let's explore these cards and their meanings and uses.

The Minor Arcana

The minor arcana has a total of fifty-six cards. Not unlike contemporary playing cards, these cards are divided into four suits of fourteen cards each. These cards are numbered accordingly. For each suit, there are ten numbered cards and four court cards. The court cards are like poker cards as well, consisting of Kings, Queens, Knights and Pages. The suits are similar to current playing cards but not the same. Traditional suits in the Italian system are coins, batons, swords and cups. Some decks have different suits depending on the theme of the deck, and wands may replace batons or pentacles may replace coins.

The Major Arcana
The cards in the major arcana are often referred to as trump cards. This group consists of twenty-two cards with no suits. Each card is individual and has its own personality and story, each numbered in the order that follows:

1.	The Fool
I.	The Magician
II.	The High Priestess
III.	The Empress
IV.	The Emperor
V.	The Hierophant
VI.	The Lovers
VII.	The Chariot
VIII.	Strength
IX.	The Hermit
X.	Wheel of Fortune
XI.	Justice
XII.	The Hanged Man
XIII.	Death
XIV.	Temperance
XV.	The Devil
XVI.	The Tower
XVII.	The Star
XVIII.	The Moon
XIX.	The Sun
XX.	Judgement
XXI.	The World

This list may seem confusing, but we will take a look at each individual card and its traditional meaning and use. The tarot is just as complicated as numerology or astrology, and when combined these arts make for a power practice of self-empowerment and mysterious insight into worlds unknown to humans with the use of only our five senses. Let's explore these cards with a more in-depth look:

1. The Fool – Innocence, curiosity, joy and freedom are represented by the fool card. This card is numbered zero to represent the ability to go in any direction at any given time.

I. The Magician – This card is representative of consciousness and creation. Manifesting your desires and direction in life. This card symbolizes creativity and internal expressions.

II. The High Priestess – The deep, dark side of a female archetype, this card represents intuition, the subconscious and the power of the moon. This inner wisdom is inherent

III. The Empress – This card represents a friendlier more welcoming side of the female archetype. Maternal instincts and unconditional love prevail. This passionate card is emotional and joyous.

IV. The Emperor – Social order and power over civilizations are represented by the emperor. Whether used for good or bad this law imposing emperor builds walls and creates boundaries

V. The Hierophant – Religious beliefs and hierarchies are governed by the Hierophant. Traditions in the occult and other esoteric knowledge are upheld by this card, offering illuminated wisdom and possibility.

VI. The Lovers – This card is as complicated as love itself, representative of connection on all levels. This connection is the creative web that holds the universe together. New beginnings and long-held passions are all aspects of this love.

VII. The Chariot – This card represents the combination of powers. Not unlike a chariot itself, it is useless without the combined efforts of man and beast. How and when skills are used, as well as strong will power are represented in this trump card.

VIII. Strength – Trump card number 8 represents the balance of opposites and being able to see this balance and use it wisely and for a just reason. Strength refers to not only physical strength but also strength of the mind and heart.

IX. The Hermit – Introspection and contemplation are aspects of this card. Mindful meditation and self-reflecting on the mysteries of life. This may not be the extrovert's favorite card, but a break from society is always a nice change of pace.

X. Wheel of Fortune – This card represents destiny and fate. Any time you hear about luck or fortune, this is the card in question. Lightly treading through life and contemplation on the effects of your past actions are built into this card.

XI. Justice – This card is just as it seems, justice on all levels, social, personal and universal. A righteous and just path is key to a morally upstanding life. Drawing this card may mean justice is coming your way, for better or for worse.

XII. The Hanged Man – Major life changes and pivotal moments come with this complicated card. Whether it's subtle or dramatic, changes are coming and you need to analyze the situation thoroughly before moving onward.

XIII. Death – This card gets a bad reputation, but symbolic death can be positive. The death of an addiction or bad habit, or even representative of the cycle of life and death. Do not fear this card; it simply means the end of something.

XIV. Temperance – This card is representative of abilities to patiently solve pressing issues and remain calm in the face of adversity. This card beckons you to stay alert, assertive and balanced as to not lose grip in the situation at hand.

XV. The Devil – This is another card with a negative reputation. Although the story of the devil has been misconstrued intentionally, this card is representative of free will and the freedom to do what one pleases. This attitude may lose your friends, but you are truly free.

XVI. The Tower – This card can represent the falling of structurally sound barriers. These walls need to be broken, regimes overthrown and rules changed. This is needed for progression, both social and personal.

XVII. The Star – The star card is hopeful and faithful; it can be a guiding light in the darkness and a balancing energy when needed most. This card is typically associated with positive representations and offers a helping hand in trying times.

XVIII. The Moon – This card is in depth just like the fluidity if the moon itself. She offers a mirror to peer into our darkest self. This is not a negative thing; we need to analyze ourselves even if we don't like what we see.

XIX. The Sun – This card represents the powerful energy of life. This vitality is the essence of all being and makes life possible. At its most unbalanced this card can be a blinding light or dehydrating heat.

XX. Judgement – This card represents time; no one can escape time and eventually will be judged in their contribution to society. This card asks that you spend your time wisely and dedicate your life to justice and redemption.

XXI. The World – This card is the final card in the major arcana. It represents an end goal that has been achieved and successfully presented to the world. It could even mean that you have found your calling and are living it in the now.

History

The roots of the tarot are quite mysterious. Some believe the tarot was introduced into modern society through nomadic cultures and travelling wise men and women who practice the occult arts. As far as the official timeline is concerned this art stems from playing cards that come to Europe from Egypt. This was thought to have taken place in the 14th century, and the cards were suited similar to the current suits of playing cards. The first documentation of tarot is dated between 1440 and 1460 in Italy, here we see the trump cards and images added to the four suit packs.

There are descriptions of packs containing images of ancient Greek gods and different types of birds. These early decks were painted and certainly haven't stood the test of time. There have been recent resurgence in demand for early decks, including the Sola-Busca tarot and its violent and darker themes. Once the printing press was invented, cards were produced on a much larger scale. As the tarot began moving its way around Europe the most popular form was the Tarot of Marseilles from Milan, this deck remains one of the most popular used today for divination, along with Aleister Crowley's THOTH Tarot and Pamela Coleman-Smith's deck often referred to as the Rider-Waite deck since it was published by the Rider Company and featured a descriptive booklet written by occultist A.E. Waite.

Once the printing press was invented, we see playing cards created in abundance for many different games. The divinatory tarot was left to the shadows as the Christian church denounced divination and other magical arts. Today we see new tarot decks being created every year, some designed by occultist for specific divination use and others dawning elves, cats, celebrities and a slew of other themes. Regardless of theme the tarot is seeing a resurgence as of late and shows no signs of slowing down.

Practice

There are infinite ways to use a tarot deck for forecasting and divination. Some people use intricate rituals and well thought out practices to commune with spirits and higher intellectual faculties of the mind. Others may simply ask a question and quickly draw a random card to gain insight. However, you go about your practice, the main act that is going to find you a successful tarot session is to 'listen' to the cards. Open your heart and mind to the images and power of the numbers. Really read your cards, learn them, get to know their personalities just as you would the planets or base numbers in numerology.

You can do readings for yourself or others. You can read for an upcoming journey or job interview. You can essentially ask the card any question, but there are specific spreads for specific areas of life, such as money or love: the more complicated the spread, the more in-depth results you will receive.

It is recommended that if you have a new to tarot to familiarize yourself with your deck. Shuffle the deck and then, one at a time, draw the top card. Focus on imagery and see if the card speaks to you. Before researching what the card traditionally means, define it yourself and see what comes to mind. This practice helps you learn to 'hear' the cards and read them on your own.

It also helps to relax the mind before you do a tarot spread. Have a designated table where you practice tarot, also have a routine. You can light incense or candles to set the mood, do some deep breathing and really clear your mind, so there isn't a distraction from what the cards are telling you. Having this routine is similar to a ritual, you sort of prepare the mind and open yourself to the cards before even handling them. Let's take a look at some popular spreads below.

Celtic cross Spread
This spread is one of the oldest spreads still in popular use today. It is a ten-card spread and is a powerful and advanced spread that can help with the most complicated of situations or questions. This is the most complicated spread in this book and is probably one of the most commonly used in the world. It can be read in a number of ways, with many combinations to be discovered.

You will begin by clearing the mind, shuffle the cards and focus fully on the question or person at hand. Ask the question or simply begin the technique. Follow the instructions below.

Draw the first card and place in front of you.

Draw the second card and place it across the first card.

Place the third card to the right of these two.

Place the fourth card below the first.

Place the fifth card above the first

Place the sixth to the left of the first.

Then, one at a time, draw four more cards placing them to the right of card number three, each one above the other.

Each of these cards will have a distinct meaning, but take a moment to read into the numerology of cards 1-10 and how they may relate to the numerology learned in this book. Below are what areas of life each card represents.

2. This card is the situation as a whole
3. This card is what is going to help or hurt the situation at hand.
4. This card represents subconscious influence, and your true desires.
5. This card represents past situations that affect the act at hand.
6. This card represents your conscious desire and how it affects the task.
7. This card represents where you are going.
8. This card is your mindset and attitude toward the situation.
9. This card represents an energetic influence.
10. This card is revealing things that are unknown to you.
11. This card represents the final outcome and connects with the 5th card.

Love Spread

This spread can be used for any romantic situation, your current relationships, past relationships and even future ones. This is a six card spread used for quick insight into where your loving companionship is going and whether or not to pursue certain loves. If there is an issue with a loved one, you can use this spread to evaluate it.

Draw the first card and place is to the top left of your tarot space.

Draw the second and place it to the right of the first card.

Draw the third card and place it to the bottom left of the first card.

Draw the fourth card and place it to the right of the third card.

Draw the fifth card and place it to the right of the fourth card.

Draw the sixth card and place it below the fourth card.

Each of these cards will have a distinct meaning pertaining to your love life or the specific relationship you are reading for.

1. This card is representative of yourself and how you feel.
2. This card represents how your partner feels about you.
3. This card represents you and your partner's connection.
4. This card represents that strength of your connection.

5. This card represents weakness in your connection.
6. This card represents what needs to be focused on in the relationship and what needs to be done to maintain the love.

Success Spread
This spread is used to evaluate any problem or challenge facing you for almost any situation that you need to be successful. Success is measured in many ways, not just money, so be creative when you use this spread, it can be used for almost any situation. This is a five-card spread.

Draw the first card and place it in the middle of your tarot space.

Draw the second card and place it to the left of the first card.

Draw the third card and place it to the right of the first card.

Draw the fourth card and place it above the second card.

Draw the fifth card and place it below the second card.

Each of these cards represents certain aspects of the situation that you are reading for.

1. This card represents your obstacle in general.
2. This card represents the challenges within this obstacle
3. This card will reveal challenges that you are not aware of.
4. This card represents how new people or aspects of the situation can help you with success and growth.
5. This card represents what actions you need to take to find success for this situation.

CHAPTER 8
Forecasting

Being able to anticipate the future or see into future events has been a desirable power of the human mind for millennia. The idea that the timeline can somehow be tapped into and manipulated may seem like something out of a comic book, but these concepts have been around for all of written history. While this practice is very mysterious, it has been practiced successfully for centuries.

Have you ever felt that someone was going to call and then they call soon after you had that thought? This is a subtle taste of how we can sense the future. Somehow our minds are not subject to the confines of time the way our bodies are, this very intriguing most of the population. But how can we practice this amazing power with purpose and intellect? Some science has been used to attempt to capture these powers but rarely see consistent results.

Many tools have been used over the years to help us tap into our potential to predict future events, among them runes, tea leaves, crystals, pendulums, stones, water and of course the areas of study in this book; Numerology, astrology and tarot. These techniques have been around for thousands of years, but to what end? Science is very valuable but tends to write off these ancient practices as superstition or parlor tricks. Let's look deeper at divination and forecasting.

What is divination or forecasting?
Divination is an attempt to find meaningful insight into the future by using ritual or esoteric techniques. There are many forms as mentioned above, but the most popular are astrology and tarot, numerology being a key part of these other two arts. These forecasting systems have stood the test of time over millennia and are still used today, even in our materialist and science-driven society.

The idea of finding love, treasure, cures and other incredible things all motivated our ancestors to use divination to achieve greatness or predict catastrophe. Nostradamus comes to mind as a famous practitioner of the divinatory arts.

Defining this practice may be simple, but its practice can take a lifetime to master. These techniques require intense focus and dedication to be used to the fullest extent.

History and Use

The idea of oracles and divination is well recorded in Alexander the Great's success as he tore through Egypt. The Oracle of Amun was visited by Alexander and spoke of his success and inevitable downfall. Although Christianity forbids these practices, the Bible contains plenty of events that would fall under the category of divination. Ancient Greece and Roman mythology are filled with plenty of divinatory events. These oracles and seers were thought to be able to communicate with gods and bring back knowledge from other realms that gave insight into earthly matters. If someone had a natural talent for these communications, they would further their practice by using various tools to assist them with their communications and visions. Seers were sought out to speak of omens and weather, to make decisions on whether or not to go into battle, or even when to plant seeds for the year's harvest. This gave the oracles and seers a very powerful position with leaders, often being hired to see into the future of a reigning king or war general.

In the Middle Ages, divination is ridiculed by the Christian church and considered an evil practice. This is often seen as hypocritical since church fathers and their practices were very similar to divinatory techniques. Even kings and queens used hired seers and magicians to help time their decisions and celebrations. John Dee comes to mind as a powerful magician that used astrology and divination to help Queen Elizabeth I with her reign, even somewhat being attributed to have been a huge part of England's powerful status for centuries leading right up to today.

So we may not be trying to build a world-renowned empire with our practices, but how can we use these techniques to empower ourselves in the 21st century? Let's discuss how this forecasting may work and what actions we can take to enhance our divination practices.

Practice

There are a number of ways to practice forecasting, and some people may be more gifted than others, but all people are capable of using these abilities to help themselves or others. Consider anytime you've run into a divinatory practice. Perhaps you've seen a needle tied to a thread held above a pregnant woman's belly to forecast the gender of the child, or maybe you've driven past a palm reader's shop while driving through the city. These common practices often get passed off as only for fun, but if performed correctly and with passion, they can reveal secrets of the world that are some of the most valuable gifts known to man.

Some people may be able to simply meditate on a subject and get a clear vision of what's to come; this is rare but not unheard of. For our intents and purposes in this book, we will assume we are starting from scratch. First, let's look into some preparatory techniques to prepare the mind for messages and insight.

Meditation

Meditation as seen a rise in popularity in recent decades, this practice is some of the most simple and powerful actions you can take to control your mind and emotions. Plus, it's free and requires no tools.

There are endless amounts of meditation techniques available online, but for the most part, simply sitting and letting the thoughts come and go as they please is enough to gain insight into the power of meditation.

Here's one simple practice:

1. Sit comfortably and quietly in a place with very little distraction
2. Breath deeply and exhale, counting one.
3. Do ten deep breaths and then count backward to one again.
4. Continue this until you no longer need to count.

5. Notice how the thoughts disappear and you are only focused on breath.
6. Continue as needed until you are in a clear mindset

This seems simple, because it is, the more you practice this, the easier it is to get into that 'zone' where your mind is free of clutter. This 'zone' is the place you want to be during any divinatory practice. The clear-headedness is needed for any information to come through that isn't your brain simply throwing images at you. This works especially well before a tarot session.

Music and Sound

Some people have trouble closing out the distractions around them; this is where music or white noise comes in. By having trance-inducing music, you can block out distractions and more easily enter into the zone. Consider Indian sitar music and its droney and repetitive layers; this is specifically designed to create a distraction-free atmosphere for meditation and insight.

There are many apps and videos online that have white noise or drone sounds to induce a trance state, while in a trance you may more readily find the answers you're seeking and gain the insight you seek. You may even wish to use an instrument such as bells or singing bowls to create the sounds yourself.

Mantras and chants go well with these practices as well; if you simply hum your own noise, you may find yourself in a trance-like state. Some prefer to use affirmations or Indian style mantras such as the OM sound to add to their meditation practice.

Yoga and Movement

Yoga, dance and other arranged movement can also induce a trance-like state. Having planned motions that are complex or repetitive will allow the mind to free itself from day to day worries and needs. This is a great technique to combine with music as well.

Yoga postures and stances help to keep the body healthy as well as the mind. The more content you are with your health, the easier it will be to enter the zone, less worry, the more one-pointedness.

Fasting

Many people have had success and incredible transformative experiences by fasting. Simply choosing a fitting day, perhaps astrologically timed, to only drink water will put the body in a heightened state of awareness, making insight and trance more easily accessible. Do your research on fasting and always listen to your body, if you are uncomfortable, then eat some fruits or other raw foods.

Combined Practice

So we now have a few preparatory practices to increase the potency of our practice. These techniques listed above are perfect for getting the mind and body ready for forecasting and divination. If we take these practices and combine them with numerology, astrology and tarot, we have a powerful combination of techniques to add to our lives and increase our success and prosperity.

What cannot be stressed enough is that for you to get the most out of these forecasting techniques is you need to listen. Being able to tell the difference between your own thoughts and cosmic insight is key to a successful practice. By practicing the preparatory techniques above and readying the mind, we will find insight and the answers we seek much easier. No one throws down some cards and gets everything they want; it comes with passion and determination, dedication and humility, and overall comes with love, for yourself and the universe.

Let's take what we have now learned and combine it all together into a formidable practice and philosophy. The next chapter is the final chapter and will connect the dots of all these powerful and ancient techniques.

CHAPTER 9
Numerology, Astrology and Tarot: The Connection

So we've made it to the final chapter, I know there's a lot to take in for such a small book, but with time, and practice, these practices will all come together to form a solid spiritual practice. Keep in mind these techniques can be customized to suit your needs; you may only want to try tarot at first, then move onto astrology, this is totally fine. You are here to empower yourself, go at your own pace and don't be overwhelmed by the complexity. The true nature of reality could not be so beautiful and simple simultaneously.

So how can we connect numerology, astrology and tarot? We have seen that numerology is inherent in all things. We have seen that the planets play an integral role in all events on earth. And we see that a tarot deck is the most useful tool for forecasting and divination. Now let's combine their powers to create a practice that has infinite potential to transform your life and create prosperity and success.

Let's start with an example of an in-depth and complex ritual that uses these techniques altogether. To reiterate, you make your own practice; this is simply an example to clarify the way these arts are connected. For this particular forecasting session, we are going to use career prospects as the desired goal. We will also assume that you have practiced and studied this book for a short period of time. Let's say we are seeking insight into what our calling is, and how we should go about achieving a favorable career.

First, we need to choose a favorable day for this particular session, study your natal chart and the current chart of planet placement. We will want a day that is ruled by Jupiter since he governs prosperity, this day is Thursday. Make sure Jupiter is not in retrograde and if possible is exalted in Cancer. If possible choose a Thursday that is in sync with your life path number, so if you're a 6 pick a Thursday that is a 6, 15 or 24. If this isn't possible try a Thursday that is Jupiter's number, 3, 12, 21 or 30. It is also recommended that you make sure that your natal Jupiter position isn't in a negative aspect with any planet that may interrupt our plans, like Uranus or Saturn transit, luckily these planets move slowly and more than like aren't transiting your natal Jupiter.

Once we have our date picked out, we can ready ourselves for the big day, preparing our mind with casual meditation and contemplation during the days or weeks leading up to the special date.

You awake on the day of your in-depth session, today you will be fasting, that is no solid foods. This can be viewed as a sacrifice to let the forces at work know you are serious about your endeavor. Awake and have some water, turn off any phones and avoid technology for this day. If possible, spend the day alone, quietly focused on your ritual. We need to shower and have a clean area to perform our ritual in, free from distraction and electronics if possible. Find out when the hour of Jupiter is that day, typically daybreak, around noon or dusk, use an app to know the exact times. You can choose one of these hours or even all three for optimum energy. For this example, we will use all three since Jupiter's number is 3.

In the morning in the hour of Jupiter, light a purple candle and leave offerings in your tarot space. Water, rum and a small amount of money, such as a dollar, will suffice. Light some incense and go into a meditative trance, visualizing Jupiter and asking for guidance. Spend as much of the hour in this space, focusing your energy on Jupiter and his numerological 3. Once you are finished, blow out the candle and continue with your quiet day.

Around midday when the hour of Jupiter has come again, return to your space for another offering and light a new purple candle, again meditate and listen in to Jupiter and his jolly benevolence. If you would like, do your breathing in groups of 3. Essentially the more things you can do in threes, the better for this example. Spend as much time as possible in this space for this hour. Once you are finished, blow out the candle and continue with your quiet day.

In the evening when the third hour of Jupiter arrives, return to your space, get a new candle, now you have three, light all three. Leave more offerings and ask Jupiter for guidance. Go into a meditative state and clear your mind. Once you feel clear, get your tarot deck and shuffle them patiently and lovingly. Ask for the deck to assist you with your career path, have a specifically worded question prepared and ask the deck to answer. Use the 'success' spread described above and slowly draw the cards. Be thoughtful and let the cards speak to you, let the energy was over you and really listen in. Once you have the spread gaze upon it and see what cards have been revealed. This reading will offer insight into your question, spend as much time in this space as possible.

Once you are finished, leave the candles burning and thank Jupiter and offer him to stay with you as long as he'd like. Be very aware of your dreams that night as well, sometimes that's where it's easiest to receive answers. But for the most part, spend the rest of the evening contemplating your spread and the experiences you had. You may not receive information right away, but be patient and open.

This is only one example of infinite combinations for these arts. Obviously, this day-long ritual will not be possible for everyone, do what you can and always listen to your heart and be open to the forces at work. We see here how these arts all interconnect to form a powerful practice that is sure to bring success.

CONCLUSION

Thank you for making it through to the end of *Numerology Awakening*, let's hope it was informative and able to provide you with all of the tools you need to achieve your goals.

The next step is to continue your practice, experiment with what you've learned to understand better what works best for you. These techniques are not simple one and done arts, as you experience the effects you are going to want to further your practice to its fullest potential. Feel free to try these practices in all aspects of life, money and love are important, but use your newfound skills to help others as well.

Numerology, astrology and tarot are ancient practices that remain powerful today. If we can further their potential and help promote their practice, we can lead society to a more spiritual and balanced state. Compassion and grace come along with these practices, just like the beautiful dance of the heavens or the depth of emotion in the art of tarot, we as humans are complex and beautiful creatures, just waiting to discover the true nature of reality.

Finally, if you found this book useful in any way, a review on Amazon is always appreciated!

DESCRIPTION

Do you wish to discover the true nature of reality? Have you seen patterns in numbers and wondered why you always see the same digits no matter where you are? Then this book has found you for a reason! *Numerology Awakening* contains everything you need to know about numbers and how they interact in our personal lives and influence the events of the world. In this book you will learn:

- The personalities of the base nine numbers
- Historical context of numerology
- How numerology relates to astrology
- How numerology relates to tarot
- Where these practices came from
- Techniques to empower yourself with these arts
- Ways to find love using these arts
- Paths to prosperity using these arts
- Practices to balance your life
- How to reveal the true nature of reality
- How to help others with these arts
- How ancient cultures used these techniques
- How modern society uses these techniques
- How to improve yourself and the world around you

If the mysterious and ancient practices of numerology, astrology and tarot have been calling to you, then get this book today!

www.ingramcontent.com/pod-product-compliance
Lightning Source LLC
Chambersburg PA
CBHW071504070526
44578CB00001B/436